THE THIRD
DIMENSION

to Charles
with Love

Dad

THE THIRD DIMENSION

Rex Humbard

FLEMING H. REVELL COMPANY
OLD TAPPAN, NEW JERSEY

Scripture quotations in this volume are from the *King James Version* of the Bible.

The poem "Your Place" by John Oxenham is used by permission of T. Oxenham.

Library of Congress Cataloging in Publication Data

Humbard, Rex,
    The third dimension.

      1. Evangelistic sermons. 2. Sermons, American.
I. Title.
BV3797.H745   252   72–4223
ISBN 0–8007–0549–1

To our four wonderful children:
Rex, Jr.
Don
Elizabeth
and
Charles

Contents

THE THIRD
DIMENSION

1

The Third Dimension

*Now Naaman, captain of the host of the king of Syria,
was a great man with his master, and honourable, because by him the Lord had given deliverance unto
Syria: he was also a mighty man in valour, but he was
a leper.*   2 Kings 5:1

We are living in the greatest civilization the world has ever
known. There are more people living today than have lived and
died in all the years since Adam and Eve. Just think about what
that means: if every person who ever lived should come out of
the grave and stand upon the face of the earth today, the number
would not equal today's population.

With this fact comes the great burden and responsibility of the
Church, of people of faith, for the souls of men! The responsibility is greater in this one generation than in all the combined
generations of Abraham, Isaac, and Jacob; of Peter, Paul, James,
and John; of Luther, Finney, and all other men of God. The
combined responsibility of all these men of the past for the souls
of mankind, cannot compare to the responsibility of this present
generation. But at this moment our world is far from the point
where God wants us to be. Why is this so? There is a reason!

Let us look for a moment at this creature we call man.

First of all, man is mental; but he is not all mind. Man is
physical; but he is not just a body. Man is spiritual, he has a

11

soul; but he is not all spiritual. He is a composite of mind, body, and soul—mental, physical, and spiritual.

Man has attained great heights, mentally. He has progressed a long way in the physical being. But he has failed—utterly failed—in developing the moral fiber of the spiritual man. That is what I want to talk about—the Third Dimension.

Go back in your imagination many hundreds of years. You will see city streets all lined with excited people. It looks like a great parade is about to take place, and everyone is eagerly waiting. Suddenly, it happens! The king's chariot appears. Everyone stands in order to see, because the king is returning after going out to meet the great general, Naaman, who has just won another war. Leading the great parade, in the first chariot, is the king. In the second chariot is Naaman, followed by his soldiers, his warriors, and the prisoners and spoils of war.

As they enter the city, everyone cries out, "Naaman, the great general! Naaman, the mighty warrior!" His name is on the lips of all the people.

It was said that Naaman was an honorable man, a great man, and he won many wars. He had not only military power, but political power, as well. In politics, he was second unto the king. He also had great social power because of his military and political position. Everyone knew the name of Naaman. "There he is. There's his wife. There's his family!" they would say.

In addition, Naaman was a man of great financial power. He had a beautiful home, with palatial gardens and lots of servants; and the spoils of war dotted his house and lands.

And so, here he is—a great man! But one day this great man of valor had a little sore appear under the skin of his hand, a little white sore which wouldn't go away. It became infected and grew worse. It got into his bloodstream, on his other hand, on his whole body. Finally, his flesh was falling from his bones. Naaman was a great man, a man of valor—BUT, he was a leper!

Do you know that Naaman would have given his military power, his social power, his political power, and all of his wealth —he would gladly have moved out of his palace if he could have just been cleansed of leprosy. He was watching himself die, bit by bit.

The way leprosy grows and spreads is like sin. The little evil thought that is entertained becomes an evil deed. An evil deed is a sin. And sin separates a man from his God. Like the social drink that finally leads to a drunkard's grave, evil thoughts, habits, and sins come into our lives and steal, destroy, and separate us from God and His Kingdom. Sin and Satan have come to kill, to destroy, to steal.

Truly, today we enjoy the greatest civilization, with all its inventions, conveniences and possibilities. Yet, there is one thing wrong with the human race: We are sinners! We have failed in the moral fiber.

Let's look at our present civilization. In the last hundred years, what has happened? One hundred years ago, there was no electricity, there were no automobiles. I can remember, just in my lifetime, when there was no atomic or hydrogen power, no TV sets or jet planes, no radios or electric washers. Now, man has all of these conveniences and inventions. In fact, we have progressed mentally until we can calculate and send a man all the way to the moon. I never thought I would live to see the day that somebody would be walking on the moon, that, by television, I would be watching him walk and hearing him talk—a quarter of a million miles away!

But man was not only smart enough to get out there; he was smart enough to come back! All the way to the moon, then back here to the earth. But, in spite of all that brainpower, he still can't get along with his fellow man. He doesn't know how to live. That's how smart he is!

Now don't misunderstand me: I believe in education. I wish

I had more. I think that people should learn, that we should have good libraries and schools to feed our minds. But let me tell you something. If we are only mental, without the moral, or if we have weak bodies, we are in trouble. We must balance ourselves. There may be enough college professors in San Quentin prison to staff a whole university. They have Ph.D.'s, D.D.'s, and all kinds of degrees, but something went wrong!

Down in Arkansas, we used to have a fellow who was rather poor and uneducated. He would slip out at night, get into the chicken coops, and steal chickens. He finally graduated from high school and went to Little Rock and got himself a college education. He came back, got into politics—and stole the county treasury! When he was uneducated, he stole chickens; but when he got his education he ran for office and was elected county treasurer. Then he stole the treasury! The difference was in education! Let me tell you, if I had my "druthers," I would rather be in heaven, learning my A B C's, than in hell, praying in Greek or Latin for water to cool my tongue.

Still, I believe in education. My work in the development of Mackinac College on Mackinac Island in Michigan shows this. Although I don't run the college, I still enjoy some influence. The president is a born-again, God-fearing Christian man, who believes in the Bible. I have told him, "If you ever begin to doubt God's Word, you will no longer be the president. The same goes for the staff of professors. Don't allow one on the campus who doesn't believe in God, and hasn't been born again."

The students are screened, too. If they don't want to hear about God and go to chapel service, then they should go to a state university or some place else. Our school is a place where people can come and learn, and still believe in God.

As I talk about education to teachers and educators I say, "God bless you. You have a gigantic task!" But I want to tell all of you something: You can be smart—as smart as the devil—and still miss heaven. And the devil is smart!

Yes, we've come a long way mentally; we all know that! And we have also come a long way physically. I am so grateful to medical science. If I were to fall and break my arm, I would find the best bone specialist in town and say, "Doc, put those bones in place." I would use him, because he has the know-how. Then I'd say, "Lord, make them mend." A doctor can cut us open, but it takes God to make us grow back. I am grateful to the doctors, the nurses, the hospitals, for what they have done, and for what they are capable of doing, but we still depend on one, and that one is the Lord.

I am glad we have made such progress in medical science. The tiny premature babies who must live for a while in incubators would die without this know-how. They can now grow into adulthood because of medical science.

Men are mental and physical, then, but they are more than that—they are also spiritual. And here is where we fail!

Why do we have so many divorces? Why do we have juvenile delinquents? Why do we have alcoholics? Why do we have hatred and strife, wars and trouble? Because man's heart—the spiritual part of man—is not right. I want to talk about this.

We can't educate a man into the Kingdom of God. We can't educate a man and make him right. He will be right only when he receives the Spirit of God. And I am old-fashioned enough to believe the Bible, that God made man, breathed into him, and man became a living soul. I don't believe he came from a monkey, though men are really making monkeys of themselves today. I am simple enough to believe that God created man and placed him in the Garden of Eden. God gave him rules and regulations by which to live, but Adam broke God's law. He was driven from the Garden, and thus lost the fellowship of God. We are a fallen race, according to the Scriptures; we are born and shaped in iniquity. Every one of us has sinned and every one of us needs a Saviour.

Now, the Bible says that a woman that liveth in pleasure is dead while she is alive (1 Timothy 5:6). What that means is that she lives in sin—transgresses God's laws. She may be a Hollywood star, she may be somebody outstanding in the community, but if she has sin in her life, then she is dead as far as spiritual things are concerned. Man is dead until he has the Spirit of God within him. If the Spirit would go out of my body today, I would have a tongue, but it wouldn't talk, my ears wouldn't hear, my eyes wouldn't see, my feet wouldn't walk, my hands wouldn't move, because the body without the spirit is dead.

It is correct to say that every member of the human race is literally dead until he has the Spirit of God, for spiritual things are spiritually understood.

Young people talk about being "turned on" by drugs. I have news for them. They don't know what "turned on" is until they have the Spirit of God come in and really "turn them on."

We can memorize every verse in the Bible, from Genesis to Revelation, but without the Spirit we cannot understand God, the Kingdom of God, or the things of God. "The letter killeth but the Spirit giveth life" (2 Corinthians 3:6).

Let us recall the incident, in John 3:1-7, concerning Nicodemus. He was a very religious man (probably more so than most of us) —a religious leader who fasted two days each week. He gave away ten percent of everything he had, even gave extra alms and offerings to help the poor and elderly, the widows and orphans. He kept every holy day, was present at every service, marched in the processional and recessional, and wore the correct robes. Physically and mentally, Nicodemus was a pillar of religion. But he was not "turned on" in the THIRD DIMENSION—spiritually.

Nicodemus came to Jesus, asking about spiritual things, and

Jesus told him, "Ye must be born again!" Nicodemus used only his head and body when he asked, "How can a man be born when he is old? can he enter the second time into his mother's womb, and be born" (John 3:4)?

The Bible says that God made man and placed him in the Garden of Eden. God gave him a law: "Of every tree of the garden thou mayest freely eat: But of the tree of the knowledge of good and evil, thou shalt not eat of it" (Genesis 2:16, 17). Adam and Eve disobeyed. They were driven from the garden, and lost God's Spirit and fellowship.

All of the Old Testament told of a Saviour and of man's being reconciled back to God. Jesus, God's only begotten Son, came into this world. He was virgin born. Mary gave Him a body, and God was His Father. Jesus' blood was from God and was therefore sinless. And Jesus proved Himself to be God manifest in the flesh. He opened blind eyes, He cast out evil spirits, He broke the loaves and fishes to feed the multitude, He raised the dead. Then He carried a cross to Calvary and fulfilled the Scripture: "He bore our sins in his own body on the tree." He died for you and me. Now, we accept God's plan of salvation: "For God so loved the world, that he gave his only begotten Son, that whosoever believeth in him should not perish, but have everlasting life" (John 3:16). God takes us out of the fallen and sinful family of Adam, and we are born again spiritually. We are "turned on" in the Third Dimension.

Then, as the Bible says, the things we once loved we now hate. So, if you used to hang out at a bar and thought you were having a good time, after you are born again you wouldn't visit that place or go around with that crowd if they paid you a million dollars; you love something else. This new life will make you go home and open your icebox, take out the liquor bottles, and empty them down the drain. It will make you pay up your debts. And the

Bible says it will make you cleanse yourself from all filthiness of the flesh *and* spirit.

I know some people whom you couldn't get to smoke, drink, lie, or steal, but their spirits are terrible; they will cut down their neighbors something awful, with their tongues. God said, "Cleanse yourself from all filthiness of the flesh and spirit." So, when a man is born again, old things pass away, and behold all things become new. If you join the church but old things have *not* passed away, then you haven't been born again; you have turned over a new leaf. But a man must be born again ("turned on" spiritually) to understand the spiritual things of God.

Yes, we of the human race have come a long way physically. We have come a long way mentally, and thank God we have! Now, if we could only progress as much spiritually as we have mentally and physically, we would have the greatest moral awakening the world has ever known. Homes would be what they should be, the Church would be what it should be, and God's Kingdom would receive honor and glory.

The law of gravity has been here ever since we have; it was here in the days of Adam and Eve. It is a bit old-fashioned and out-of-date today, I would guess. But still, we should thank God for gravity, for it holds us to the earth and keeps us from drifting off into space. Gravity is a real blessing: That little apple up there comes down to us—it doesn't float away.

But, I tell you, go and get a good college education—progress mentally, and get smart. Keep your body strong and fit. Then, step out and say, "I have a good education, I have a body that is strong and fit. I am not bound by those old-fashioned rules and regulations, like gravity, and I am going to prove it to everybody!" Climb up on the front of a high building and jump out into space. Defy that old-fashioned law, and see what happens! That law which has been blessing you will let you go SMACK against the earth. It will curse you if you disobey it.

A man can strive to make a big fortune, but he doesn't know what he is looking for—he is not happy. And his home will not be happy, either.

The revolution that everybody wants and the way of life that everyone wants is so simple that we all just stagger right over it. Here it is:

Everybody really wants to be "turned on" spiritually, wants to understand the things of God and know that His commandments are for man's benefit, not God's. If we will keep His laws and commandments, they will bless us and our families. Our communities, our society, and our world will be happy. We will all be happy! But, if we disobey them—just as if we disobey gravity —there is a curse. What a city this would be if everybody would keep these simple commandments and laws: the Ten Commandment, the Beatitudes, and the other teachings of Jesus!

"Thou shalt not lie." Wouldn't this be a wonderful community if no one lied? "Thou shalt not steal." We could dismiss most of our police force, and our jails would be nearly empty if people wouldn't steal. "Thou shalt not commit adultery." We wouldn't have these divorce courts, so many little boys and girls suffering, families being broken up, if we kept that commandment. "Thou shalt not bear false witness." "Honor thy father and thy mother." (And dads and mothers should live so their children CAN honor them.) "Thou shalt not covet." These are the laws of God by which He told us to live. And when we do not live by them, just as when we defy the law of gravity, we are in trouble. And that is what's wrong with our human race!

We need to get back and have a moral and spiritual awakening —to "turn on" and realize, "These are God's laws; let's keep them!" "Thou shalt have no other gods before me." "Seek ye first the kingdom of God, and His righteousness; and all these things shall be added unto you." God comes first, not second, not fifteenth. "Love your neighbor as yourself." That is the revolution the world is wanting. Not everyone will accept it, but *you* can have it. And, when you do, when you keep His laws and commandments, when you are born again and "turned on," spiritually, brother, you are living in another world! There is no one like a real, born-again, Spirit-filled Christian. No one!

Use your brain, then, take care of your body, and be "turned on" spiritually.

Now, how did Naaman get well? The same way we can get "turned on" spiritually. Three steps! Naaman acknowledged he was a leper. The flesh was falling from his bones. His wife knew he was a leper. Their little maid knew he was a leper. The king knew he was a leper. He admitted he was a leper. Our first step, in "turning on" spiritually is to acknowledge that we have sinned. We will never get a thing from God until we admit our need. Our self-righteousness is as filthy rags when we come to be born again. Only Christ can give us His Spirit. That's number one: Naaman acknowledged he was a leper.

Second, Naaman went to the source of his help. We must go to the source of *our* help—which is to Calvary. Receive Christ, and receive His Spirit!

When Naaman went to the king, the king got mad and said, "You are trying to declare war!" But Elisha said, "Let him come now to me." So Naaman went down to the prophet's house. The prophet knew he was a high, haughty, rich man, used to getting whatever he wanted. As a result, he had to be cut down a little bit.

When we come to Calvary, we can't come with social pull, political pull, financial pull. We just have to come like everybody else. We have ALL sinned.

The prophet of the Lord knew this, so he sent a messenger who told Naaman to go down and dip in the Jordan River seven times if he wanted to get well. Naaman went into a rage. "Who does he think he is?" he said. "He didn't come out to salute me, or bow down to me. Don't tell me to go down and get in that old muddy water! Why, the rivers in Syria are clear. I'll go back up there and wash."

So Naaman got sidetracked, just like a lot of people do today with various doctrines, issues, schisms, and denominational differences.

But I want to tell you something: We must come only in God's way, and if we don't come in God's way, we won't get God's answer. So don't get sidetracked like Naaman. Go back to Calvary, to Jesus.

Naaman tried to go another way. He got in his chariot and started home. But a little buck private got up and said, "Your honor, if the prophet had told you to do some great thing, you would have done it, wouldn't you? Since he said only 'wash and be clean,' shouldn't you at least give it a try?" Naaman saw his folly, and he went down to the Jordan. Did he dip five times, then go away and say "It's not as good as he said?" No, God had said seven times, and when Naaman came up the seventh time old things had passed away, and behold, all things had become new: He had flesh like a little child's.

Sometimes people come to my church and then go home and say, "Rex said it was good and I would get 'turned on' but it didn't happen."

No, if we are not willing to clean out our iceboxes, to clean up our ungodly lives, if we are not willing to give up our sins and bad habits—the wrong things we are doing and saying, it will never happen. We have to come clean with God.

People come to the altar and bounce down on one knee, bounce back up and say, "I'm a Christian." I've news for them. There's a lot more to it than that. They have to come clean with God and give up their sins and turn from their evil ways. Only then will they have a real spiritual birth.

We have to go all the way. The Lord knows the thoughts that are going through our minds. He knows every act of our lives.

When we deal with Him, brother, He knows all! We can't hide anything from God. We can join a church and fool the preacher, but it is not the preacher we are going to meet in judgment—it is the Lord!

Now, we don't have a bunch of angels in the Cathedral of Tomorrow. I thank God we have hypocrites here—we have people who need something. If there is anything a hypocrite should do, it is go to church, so he can hear the Word of God.

When Naaman saw that his leprosy was gone he said, "Look, God made me well!" He told everyone.

When we repent and are baptized (Mark 16:16), and "turn on" spiritually, in the Third Dimension, we know it! Our families know it! Our neighbors know it! The fellows at the shop know it! We don't have to put up a big sign which says, "I'm a Christian." We just act like Christians, because we are Christians!

"YE MUST BE BORN AGAIN." You must "turn on" spiritually!

2

Faith

Now faith is the substance of things hoped for, the evidence of things not seen. For by it the elders obtained a good report. Through faith we understand that the worlds were framed by the word of God, so that things which are seen were not made of things which do appear. Hebrews 11:1-3

In order to develop the all-important Third Dimension we talked about in Chapter One, we must grow in faith. Now, faith is the substance of the title deed of things hoped for. Our faith is our title deed to eternal life. Suppose I had a piece of property and I came to you with the deed and said, "Look here, I have a deed to a piece of property." Suppose you would reply with, "But I don't see the property. Where's the property? I don't believe you have any."

Now there is not a single person, who knows anything about legal papers, who—if I had a real deed which had been legally authorized, stamped, registered, etc.—would disbelieve or question such a deed when I showed it to him.

The title deed to eternal life is our faith. We have eternal life if we have faith in Jesus Christ, faith in God's plan of salvation, and faith in the Word of God. We can see by faith something which is not seen. "While we look not at the things which are seen, but at the things which are not seen . . ." (2 Corinthians 4:18). This is

23

faith! It is our title deed to the promises of God and to eternal
life, just like a deed is the title to property which we may own.
Faith is taking God at His word and asking no questions. "But
without faith it is impossible to please him: for he that cometh to
God must believe that he is, and that he is a rewarder of them
that diligently seek him" (Hebrews 11:6).

People who say, "I have faith, but I cannot understand . . . I
have faith, but I cannot see," do not have Bible-believing faith.
Faith takes God at His word. That is real faith! Faith is knowing
that all things work together for good to them that love God, to
them who are the called according to his purpose (Romans 8:28).
All things work together—now, that means *all* things.

Don't misunderstand. Faith does not believe that all things
are good. For example, no one would get up in church and
say, "We were driving to church and we had a wreck. Glory
to God!" We don't glory because we have a wreck; we don't
glory because things sometimes go wrong; but we have faith
in God that we are His children and that He is watching over
us. We know that He is taking care of us and that everything will
come out all right. It may take eternity to reveal this to us, but if
we love the Lord, we are on the winning team. We may lose a
scrimmage here and there; we may end up with some knocks and
bumps, but if we have faith in God—faith in His Word—if we are
born again, I'm here to tell you that we can depend on God's
Word; Romans 8:28 is still in the Bible.

No, faith does not believe that all things are good or that all
things always work well; but it does believe that all things, good
or bad, work *together* for them that love God. Now, I like good
hot biscuits, but I don't like the biscuits before they are done. I
don't like to eat lard by itself; that's not good. I don't want to eat
the flour by itself; that's not good. I don't want the salt by itself. But
if they all are worked together properly, put in the oven and baked,
the result is good. So it is with life. Tribulation worketh patience

—and many times we are saying, "God, give me patience." Tribulation is coming, and the fire and the heat; but hold steady, be true, believe God, for all things work together for good to them that love God. Don't whine when you don't like something; wait until it is done.

Trust the Lord. Believe the Lord. Believe that He knows what is right for you. Faith has two sides: One has to do with the intellect; the other has to do with the will. By faith, the mind trusts in God, the heart responds to the love of God, and the will submits to His commands. Then, we have real faith! But, if your mind is wandering out yonder with question marks, and the will in your life is not to obey the commandments of the Lord, you can't expect to have Bible-believing faith.

Faith is paradoxical. It goes beyond reason. It believes without understanding. Faith sings, even in prison. In Acts 16:25, at the midnight hour Paul and Silas prayed and sang praises unto God, and the prisoners heard them. Faith sings in the darkest hour. It glories in tribulation—Romans 5:3: "And not only so, but we glory in tribulations also: knowing that tribulation worketh patience." It chooses to suffer—Hebrews 11:25: "Choosing rather to suffer affliction with the people of God, than to enjoy the pleasures of sin for a season." That passage is talking about Moses, who would have become a Pharaoh and a powerful man, but he chose to suffer the afflictions of the righteous for a season rather than to enjoy the pleasures of sin and the world.

Faith accepts all things as a part of God's will—Philippians 1:12: "But I would ye should understand, brethren, that the things which happened unto me have fallen out rather unto the furtherance of the gospel." We are not born with this faith; it comes by hearing the Word of God—Romans 10:17: "So then faith cometh by hearing, and hearing by the word of God." This is why we are commanded to preach the Gospel to every creature, that they might hear, that they might have faith so that they might believe—Romans 10:13, 14: "For whosoever shall call upon the name of the Lord shall be saved. How then shall they call on him in whom they have not believed? and how shall they believe in him of whom they have not heard? and how shall they hear without a preacher?"

I want you to know that my responsibility is great before God Almighty, as I preach and write about Him. And you who listen and read, your responsibility is great. "For whosoever shall call upon the name of the Lord shall be saved," and many people need to be saved. But "How then shall they call on him in whom they have not believed?" They cannot be saved if they have not believed. "And how shall they believe in him of whom they have not heard?" We have to preach, we have to tell. "And how shall they hear without a preacher?"

In Arkansas, we used to have the old-fashioned camp meetings, with the Methodists, the Baptists and the Presbyterians all together. They would cook up a big pot of beans, and they all ate together, and everyone slept in a tent or camped out. They prayed, they believed God—and revival came! But that day is gone. There was a day when we had an auditorium, a tabernacle, or a tent where we had protracted meetings and revival. But that day is gone! You can't get the sinners out. Friends, the way for revival today is through the electronic tube which everyone watches and listens to now.

You cannot live a life of victory over the world without faith—1 John 5:4: "For whatsoever is born of God overcometh the world: and this is the victory that overcometh the world, even our faith." My friend, if you have been born of the spirit and power of God, you can be an overcomer of sin, of the flesh, of the devil, and of this present world. You cannot please God without faith—Hebrews 11:6: "But without faith it is impossible to please him: for he that cometh to God must believe that he is. . . ." (you don't question; you just believe that He is) "and that he is a rewarder of them that diligently seek him." God still rewards the faithful; He is on the throne and He can and does answer prayer.

You cannot pray without faith—James 1:6: "But let him ask in faith, nothing wavering. For he that wavereth is like a wave of the sea driven with the wind and tossed." You cannot please God without faith. And there can be no peace in your heart until you have faith. "Therefore being justified by faith, we have peace with God through our Lord Jesus Christ" (Romans 5:1).

You cannot have joy without faith—1 Peter 1:8: "Whom having not seen, ye love; in whom, though now ye see him not, yet believing, ye rejoice with joy unspeakable and full of glory."

We are justified by faith and not by works—Galatians 2:16. We are to live by faith—"I am crucified with Christ: nevertheless I live; yet not I, but Christ liveth in me: . . . (Galatians 2:20). It is not you that lives your faith; you are crucified with Christ, and now Christ liveth in you. It goes on to say, "Christ liveth in me: and the life which I now live in the flesh I live by the faith of the Son of God who loved me, and gave himself for me." We are made righteous by faith, not by works, not by what we do, but by our faith in the righteous one, Jesus Christ. My heart's desire and prayer to God is that all might come to know this saving faith.

Christ rose in the heart by faith—Ephesians 3:17: "That Christ may dwell in your hearts by faith; that ye, being rooted and grounded in love, May be able to comprehend. . . ." The Holy Spirit is received by faith—"This only would I learn of you, Received ye the Spirit by the works of the law, or by the hearing of faith" (Galatians 3:2)? Whatsoever is not of faith is of sin. If we do not have faith, then we live in sin. So many people today seem to think they are going to go to heaven because they never robbed any banks, killed anybody, or ran off with another man's wife. That doesn't mean that one is a person of faith. Whatsoever is not of faith is of sin—Romans 14:23: "And he that doubteth is damned if he eat, because he eateth not of faith: for whatsoever is not of faith is sin."

Faith is important because it honors God, and God always honors faith. I am glad for that.

Now, take the subject of "little faith." You remember how Jesus came walking on the water and Peter looked out there and said, "Lord, if it's you, let me come." He climbed out of the boat and started walking on the water. But Peter looked at the waves whipped up by the wind, and he became afraid. Then he began to sink and cried out, "Lord, save me!" And Christ said, "Oh, thou of little faith!" Little faith!

Peter did the impossible: he walked on the water! He walked by faith! Peter also did the conceivable thing. When he saw the storm, he had a second thought, and he doubted. For a moment, he lost sight of Jesus, and at that moment he began to sink.

Peter did the natural thing here: He feared destruction. Doubt always brings fear of destruction. Then Peter did the expected thing: He began to sink. We fail when we start to doubt. Without faith, we begin to fail and when we begin to fail, we begin to sink, as far as spiritual things are concerned. But when Peter began to sink he did the right thing: He looked to Jesus and said, "Lord, save me"; and the Lord had mercy on him and saved him. Then, again, Peter did the impossible thing: Jesus took him by the hand and pulled him up and Peter walked on the water back to the boat.

Now, let us look at the steps that led to his failure. Peter started by faith and walked on the water; then he saw the storm, and he had second thoughts and began to doubt. That produced fear, and that brought about failure!

So it is in our spiritual life. We must be careful. We must hold on to our faith. There are three kinds of faith. We find them in the story of the resurrection of Lazarus (John, Chapter 11). There were Mary, Martha, and Lazarus, whom Jesus loved and whom He visited many times. Now, when Lazarus died, Mary's faith was *limited.* She said, "Lord, if thou hadst been here, my brother had not died" (John 11:32). She limited her faith to saying, "Lord, this is what I believe . . . not your will . . . not the way you work, but if you had worked the way I wanted you to work, everything would have come out all right." She limited her faith.

Martha's faith was *literal,* but went a bit beyond Mary's. When Jesus said to her, "Thy brother shall rise again," she said, "I know that he shall rise again in the resurrection. I believe that someday there will be a general resurrection." She had a basic faith to believe the Word and the Word only—*literally.* But she robbed herself by not expanding her faith.

Third, Jesus' faith was *unlimited.* He said, "He is going to rise from the dead." Then He told them to roll away the stone, and they did. This was the *unlimited faith!*

Then Jesus called, "Lazarus, come forth!"

Three kinds of faith—the kind where we place a limit on faith and the basic faith by which we rob ourselves; but I pray that we will have the unlimited faith to say that our God is able to supply all our needs, according to His riches in glory, through Christ Jesus, our Lord.

Now, no one should ever talk about faith without going to Hebrews 11:33–39, where we read: "Who through faith subdued kingdoms, wrought righteousness, obtained promises, stopped the mouths of lions, Quenched the violence of fire, escaped the edge of the sword, out of weakness were made strong, waxed valiant in fight, turned to flight the armies of the aliens. Women received their dead raised to life again: and others were tortured, not accepting deliverance; that they might obtain a better resurrection: And others had trial of cruel mockings and scourgings, yea, moreover of bonds and imprisonment: They were stoned, they were sawn asunder, were tempted, were slain with the sword: they wandered about in sheepskins and goatskins; being destitute, afflicted, tormented; (Of whom the world was not worthy:) they wandered in deserts, and in mountains, and in dens and caves of the earth. And these all, having obtained a good report through faith, received not the promise."

I tell you, this is called the hall of faith, and there are those who believe God and worship God—people who worship by faith, as Abel; who walk by faith, as Enoch; who work by faith, as Noah; who live by faith, as Abraham. There are those who have governed by faith, as Moses; they followed by faith, as Israel; they fought by faith, as Joshua; they conquered by faith, as Gideon; they subdued kingdoms by faith, as David; they walked through the fiery furnace by faith, as the Hebrew children; they suffered by faith, as Paul; and they died for their faith as Stephen, that first Christian martyr. "Looking unto Jesus the author and finisher of our faith; who for the joy that was set before him endured the cross, despising the shame, and is set down at the right hand of the throne of God" (Hebrews 12:2).

The faith of the saints inspires us, but we look to the unlimited faith of Jesus as our example!

3

When God Stirs Your Nest

As an eagle stirreth up her nest, fluttereth over her young, spreadeth abroad her wings, taketh them, beareth them on her wings: So the Lord alone did lead him, and there was no strange god with him.
Deuteronomy 32:11, 12

It's easy to have faith when everything is going along smoothly. But what happens when the road begins to get rough? At this very moment you may be passing through a difficult trial. Perhaps the burden is pressing heavily upon your heart.

I would like to remind you that an all-wise, loving Heavenly Father longs for you to simply trust Him. When your burdens are fully committed to Him, real spiritual growth is the result.

If you will look back over your life, I think you will agree that the closest you have ever been to God was during those times when you have had to pray and trust Him to see you through some heartache or difficulty. This is when we learn best that God's grace *is* sufficient.

I hope this message will strengthen your heart and encourage you in realizing anew how very great the love of the Father is concerning you.

When a parent punishes a child for being naughty, believe me, that child has a full knowledge that his parent is really close by. In this same manner, times of testing and trial will come to the children of God. They are our proving ground. The Lord doesn't forsake us at such difficult times. He is as close then as He is when we joyfully reach mountaintop experiences in our Christian walk.

"Whom the Lord loveth, he chasteneth" (Hebrews 12:6).

In the Old Testament we read of the great love God had for Moses. Now, Moses was loyal to God, but his weaknesses often caused him to make mistakes. Because of this, God allowed him to pass through severe chastenings.

One day, Moses looked up and saw a great eagle—the monarch of birds that loves to soar the heights, and builds its nest high among the rocky ledges. As he watched that eagle, God preached Moses a sermon.

The first thing the eagle did was to find a proper place for her young. She soared high onto a ledge in a rugged, desolate area, away from everything that would harm or be dangerous to the baby eaglets. She then began the task of building a nest.

She gathered briars, sticks, and sharp pieces of wood. When this prickly framework was made, she lined it with rabbit and squirrel fur and then finally a touch of feathers, making a nice, soft, comfortable nest.

Then the eggs were laid, and finally the eaglets hatched. Everything was so warm and comfortable. Life was sure a great thing!

Together the mother and father went out and found food. They fed the eaglets until they were pleasingly plump. The young birds were developing and growing without a worry or concern.

But suddenly, the situation changes. The mother eagle reaches into the nest with her long beak and jerks out the lining, throwing it down over the cliff! Now the eaglets are sitting on thorns and thistles. They're uncomfortable, miserable. The nest is stirring with activity as they squirm to find a comfortable spot.

Looking up at their mother, they see her as they've never seen her before. They sense something majestic as she unfolds her great wings and flutters them above their questioning eyes. How comforting she is!

Then they begin to cry out, "Help us! You've always made us comfortable and supplied our needs before. Why don't you stop our suffering?" But even as they cry out in pain for help, they begin to think of leaving that nest.

The mother eagle has always been close by, but never closer than just now, during this time of change. She places her strong wing down on the nest and gently coaxes the frightened eaglets out onto her wing.

Then up they go into the wide blue above, up one thousand feet, then two thousand feet. Suddenly the little birds see a world they have never seen before. A big, wonderful world of wide horizons.

Almost before the eaglets know what is happening, the ride is over: The mother turns a flip-flop, sending them screaming through the air. Faced with this new situation, they spread out their wings and begin to glide, using strength they've never used before. They are soaring like their mother!

When they falter mother eagle swoops down underneath and regains them on her own wings. Patiently, she continues the process until she sees they can soar the heights without need of her assistance.

At last the eaglets have no desire to go back to the confining walls of the nest; they have discovered new horizons.

As Moses considered the lesson of the eagle, he realized the wonderful comparison of the mother eagle's love for her young and the love of God for His children. His life took on a new meaning. Today, it can do the same for us.

In this illustration we see the picture of the young convert. Having received Christ, he is born again. The joy in his heart is unspeakable. It's wonderful! He wants everyone in the whole world to know about it.

But, just as life soon changed for the eaglets, so our walk with the Lord soon encounters the rough curves of opposition and discouragement.

Many precious Christians start out with a firm belief that life is going to be rosy from there on out. The early Church experienced this. On the day of Pentecost, the Holy Ghost was poured out, and 3,000 were saved. A few days later 5,000 more were saved.

The Church was sitting there in its comfortable home in Jerusalem. They were having glorious services that thrilled the hearts of everyone present. It was wonderful to be there.

But Jesus had given the Great Commission to "go ye into all the world and preach the gospel to every creature" (Mark 16:15).

Then, in Matthew 28:19, 20, we read: "Go ye therefore, and teach all nations, baptizing them in the name of the Father, and of the Son, and of the Holy Ghost: teaching them to observe all things whatsoever I have commanded you: and, lo, I am with you alway, even unto the end of the world."

God saw a whole world that was lost, and said, "Go!" And here they sat in their comfortable pews, singing "Blessed Assurance!"

What happened? The Lord pulled the featherbed out, and the early Church became uncomfortable. Persecutions began, many of them headed by a man called Saul of Tarsus. He became famous for his work against the Church, and held the coats of those who stoned the martyr Stephen. Stephen had made a great witness for the risen Lord, but he was dragged outside the city, charged with blasphemy, and stoned to death.

Arrests of Christians continued. Many were jailed, and some were killed. There was no longer a comfortable nest.

The Christians had been content to fellowship within their

small circle, and had neglected to go into the outside world. But now, stirred by the thorns of opposition, they began to spread out—one toward Samaria, one to Damascus, and so on. They were running from persecution, but everywhere they ran, they preached the Word!

Now, this same lesson is true today. If we are sitting pleasantly within our nests, not interested whether the rest of the world goes to hell or heaven, we are not carrying out the Great Commission; we are not fulfilling our purpose as children of God.

When the child of God settles down comfortably, no one sees the glory of God radiating through that life. And so God allows him to be jabbed by the thorns of persecution and trials, that he might be stirred and develop a vision for a lost world around him.

If we could only look upon these trials as privileges, we would be able to see glimpses of their full value. The people who have really amounted to something for God have been those that God allowed to pass through the fires of opposition. They come out tried, tested—and precious in the sight of God.

When our situation is past endurance, and everything seems hopeless, then we will begin to look up. This is when we will see how great God is in our time of need.

"Why art thou cast down, O my soul? and why art thou disquieted within me? hope in God: for I shall yet praise him, who is the health of my countenance, and my God" (Psalms 43:5). "Blessed is that man that maketh the Lord his trust, and respecteth not the proud, nor such as turn aside to lies" (Psalms 40:4).

It is in the time of discouragement that we must remember God's Word, and look to His promises, "I will never leave thee, nor forsake thee" (Hebrews 13:5). "Whereby are given unto us exceeding great and precious promises: that by these ye might be partakers of the divine nature, having escaped the corruption that is in the world through lust" (2 Peter 1:4).

Happy is the man whom God corrects. "Therefore despise not thou the chastening of the Almighty" (Job 5:17).

Do we want to stay in the nest? Or can we say with Paul, "But we glory in tribulations also: knowing that tribulation worketh patience; and patience, experience; and experience, hope: And hope maketh not ashamed; because the love of God is shed abroad in our hearts by the Holy Ghost which is given unto us" (Romans 5:3–5)?

We must first have a hope that maketh not ashamed, and it is through experience that we gain hope. But experience will never come without patience. And patience is built in the midst of tribulation.

Yes! A lot of people want that hope, and want the Holy Ghost in their hearts, but they don't want to go back all the way to where it begins—with tribulations, trials and testings!

"I . . . will try them as gold is tried: they shall call on my name, and I will hear them: I will say, It is my people: and they shall say, The Lord is my God" (Zechariah 13:9).

There is another illustration that can help us in our understanding of life's difficult places. I heard it many years ago and would like to share it with you now.

If you were to go to the store and buy a little jar of pear preserves, take them out of the jar, and put them on a plate, they would still be preserves a week later. But if you did the same thing with just a plain pear, it wouldn't work that way.

A lot of things happen before pears become preserves. First, someone removes all the little specks and brown spots with a knife. Then they are peeled. But they are not preserves yet; there is more to be done. They must be quartered and cored—and still the work is not completed.

Then the pears are put in a pan, and sugar is added. The pan is put on the fire and the mixture is cooked.

Those pears are now saturated through and through. They can be taken out of the pan and they will be preserves on the table, in the garbage can—anywhere, because they have a lasting power on the inside. But it didn't come easy.

The saint of God, converted, sanctified, Spirit-filled, is still not through with the testings. Our training is just beginning.

I am sure you want to be fully preserved until the Lord comes. Then learn this wonderful lesson that God taught Moses: Learn to glory in tribulation, knowing that tribulation worketh patience, experience, and hope.

God is having His perfect will and way in your life when He gives you the privilege of a tried and tested life. You are a chosen vessel, and He desires that you may shine as gold and be used unto His honor.

When blessings seem to be taken away and trials set in, exercise your faith. Flap your wings a little bit. God is near, and will not suffer you to be tempted above that which you are able to bear.

The eagles did not fight off the mother bird who offered help in the midst of the learning process. Neither do we dare turn our backs on God in our time of need. Don't refuse His help. Let yourself become aware of His steadfast concern and love for you.

"But they that wait upon the Lord shall renew their strength; they shall mount up with wings as eagles; they shall run, and not be weary; and they shall walk, and not faint" (Isaiah 40:31).

If you are going through a trial, experiencing illness or heartache, knowing disappointment, may you just now claim this text for yourself: "The Lord alone did lead him, and there was no strange god with him."

He whose eye is on even the tiny sparrow is your God!

4

Putting God First in the Home

Therefore shall a man leave his father and his mother, and shall cleave unto his wife: and they shall be one flesh. Genesis 2:24

Just as the mother eagle protects her young, but also sees that they develop the ability to take care of themselves, so every member of a Christian home should protect and encourage the others in that home.

Marriage is beautiful! It is the coming together of a man and a woman. They delight in one another's company and, by publicly exchanging vows, testify before God and the world that they want to be joined together for life. They no longer desire to go their separate ways, but are interested in the common call of establishing their own home.

God's Word has much to say about the responsibilities of the man and wife after they have "tied the knot." And I should like to focus your attention on the importance of fulfilling these responsibilities by putting God first in the home.

A home that denies God is not really a home. It may have the physical appearance of a home, but it is not a real home if it does not have God as its center. I don't care if you are a common laborer or the president of a huge corporation, if you do not know God and put Him first in your life and home, your life will be a total failure, and your home will be an unhappy one.

The home was instituted by God, not man. It is to be a place of peace and tranquility, shut off from the roar of the world outside the door. God in His infinite knowledge knew that every family member needed a place of refuge to restore his body and to be contented, knowing he was loved by other members of the family. The home was intended to be the foundation for the instruction of God's Word, a place where children would be taught "the fear and admonition of the Lord."

But, how many homes operate the way God intended them to? You must ask yourself: "Am I living the way I ought to live? Would I want my children walking in my footsteps? Have I trained up my child in the way he should go so that when he grows old he will not depart from it?" Don't forget, children learn by observing their elders.

A six-year-old boy and his father were speeding down the highway when they were stopped by a police car. Dad said, "Look, I'm in a hurry, here's five dollars to forget the whole thing." The officer put the money in his wallet and said to himself, "It's okay to take a bribe; everyone else is doing it."

When the boy was eight, he listened while his uncle reported to the adults at the dinner table how he had cheated a little on his income tax. "Everyone is doing it" said the uncle.

When the boy was 12 years old he got into a fight and broke his glasses. His aunt called the insurance company and claimed they were lost so they could collect the money needed to buy another pair. "Everyone does it," she said.

At the age of 16 the boy got a part-time job in a supermarket and heard the manager say, "Put these over-ripe tomatoes in the bottom of the basket. It's all right—everyone does it."

When he was 19, he entered college. His roommate offered to sell him the questions for an important test. "Sure, why not?" said the boy. "Everyone else does it." But he was caught and expelled from the college. At home his dad was furious. "How could you do such a thing to us?" he shouted.

If there is one thing adults can't stand, it is a child who cheats. But Dad and Mom, I say to you, if they see you wink at the law, they will do the same. If they see you drinking, they are going to do it, too. If you swear and lie, they will swear and lie. It's time for parents to stop demanding something from their children that they don't practice themselves.

At this hour the world is suffering because the home has fallen into decay. There is hardly a nation, city or community where crime does not abound on every hand. Here in America we have all types of people trying to analyze the problem. The psychiatrist, the sociologist, the economist and the politician are all chasing after the answers.

It reminds me of a cartoon I once saw in a Vermont newspaper. It pictured a mechanic working on an automobile. Parts were scattered all over the garage floor when his buddy inside the car yelled, "Hey, I found the trouble. It's out of gas!"

That's the picture today. Most of the people are running around, tearing things apart, trying to find the trouble. I know what the trouble is: We are out of God!

We must put God back into the home if we are to overcome in these troubled times. And in order to do this, Mom and Dad must take their responsibility and make the place where they live truly a home.

A child, like an adult, has 8,760 hours a year to use. If he averages eight hours of sleep a night he still has 5,840 waking hours. Counting three hours each week for Sunday school and church, he still has 5,684 hours left. School will take another 1,080 hours, and that leaves the child with 4,604 hours of free time. These are the hours that should be under the direct supervision of the home.

In light of these facts, where does the responsibility for

training children lie? Obviously in the home, where the greatest amount of time is spent. And when a child goes wrong, we must reflect back on the fact that, in most cases, it was the home that went wrong in the first place.

The place to reform the world, then, is not in the electric chair, but in the high chair. The place to teach respect and obedience to authority is not in the state pen, but in the playpen. The time to save people is not after they find that the wages of sin is death, but before.

In 1855 the United States was acknowledged as one of the most law-abiding nations in the world. One hundred years later, the American Bar Association declared that it was the most criminal nation on the face of the earth. Everyone asks, "What went wrong?" Trace the problem back, and you find a moral breakdown in the family and home.

It is time for us to reestablish faith and the principles of God in our lives and in our homes. If its homes fail, the country's entire foundation will crumble and fall away. We need an old-fashioned, Holy Ghost, saving revival in the homes of America. We must make our homes places where dads will be dads, where mothers will be mothers, and children will be the children that they ought to be, standing in the Presence of God, and keeping His commandments. Then, God's blessings will rest upon them.

Deuteronomy 29:9-13 promises this: "Keep therefore the words of this covenant, and do them, that ye may prosper in all that ye do. Ye stand this day all of you before the Lord your God; your captains of your tribes, your elders, and your officers, with all the men of Israel, Your little ones, your wives, and thy stranger that is in thy camp, from the hewer of thy wood unto the drawer of thy water: That thou shouldest enter into covenant with the Lord thy God, and into his oath, which the Lord thy God maketh with thee this day: That he may establish thee to day for a people unto himself, and that he may be unto thee a God, as he hath said unto thee, and as he hath sworn unto thy fathers, to Abraham, to Isaac, and to Jacob."

A family altar, or a devotional time with the family gathered around, should be just as much a part of a Christian home as eating. Learning from the Word of God is necessary for the entire family. And parents are particularly told to teach the Word to the children and to set examples: "And thou shalt teach them diligently unto thy children, and shalt talk of them when thou sittest in thine house, and when thou walkest by the way, and when thou liest down, and when thou risest up" (Deuteronomy 6:7).

A minister, making pastoral calls, visited a farm family of his congregation. He found the farmer's wife busy in the kitchen, washing up the cream separator. The sink was piled high with the many stainless steel parts, and the minister, knowing the ways of farm life, insisted she continue with her work while they talked of church matters.

Suddenly, her little boy popped into the room with an open magazine. "Mama," he asked courteously, "what does this picture mean?"

The mother laid aside the cream separator parts, washed and dried her hands, and sat down at the kitchen table with her son. She patiently answered each of his questions. Finally satisfied, the youngster left the room, happy.

"I see why your children are so polite and why they love you so much," commented the minister.

The farmer's wife, back at the sink again, replied, "I guess I'll always be washing cream separators, but never again will my son ask me that particular question."

It's time we examine our values. What is the most valuable thing in the world after you have God in your life and in your home? Is the family God entrusted to you more important than cream separators? More important than being president of a company? More important than money in the bank?

Love and genuine interest pay uncountable dividends to all members of a family. Scripture tells us in Romans 12:10, "Be kindly affectioned one to another. . . ." Don't demand all for yourself, but honor each other and prefer that others in the family should be happy. It works two ways; you can't sprinkle perfume on someone without getting a little on yourself.

This is just as important for husbands and wives as it is for parents and children. Many times the husband gets so wrapped up in his work that when he comes home he hardly gives his wife the time of day. Wives, too, can be so involved in keeping the house immaculate that when their husbands return from work the only thing they can say is, "Take your shoes off before you go into the living room. I just finished cleaning the rug."

Don't nag at each other. If your husband wants to play golf and you don't, let him go, and tell him to hurry home. Smile at him when you say it, and he'll come back a lot quicker. And men, if your wives want to do a little window shopping and you don't, let them go without complaining about how long it takes. There should be mutual respect between husband and wife.

Don't get overly in debt. Many are having a hard time in their homes because they are like the young man who decided he had to have a nice big house, the most powerful car, and the most expensive wardrobe.

After a while, he got out his pencil and figured out that his time payments totalled three times his salary! You can buy your way right into trouble, like he did, and it will reflect upon your home.

A home that does not have unity is a home that needs to get back to God. The Bible admonishes us in Mark 3:25, "If a house be divided against itself, that house cannot stand." In Ephesians 5:25 it says, "Husbands, love your wives, even as Christ also loved the church, and gave himself for it." And in Titus 2:4, "That they may teach the young women . . . to love their husbands, and to love their children."

Many homes today are in turmoil, on the verge of collapse— Dad against Mother, children against parents, fighting and bickering at every hand. The only answer is for each member to repent. It's time for dads, mothers, boys and girls to stand before the Lord and say, "Lord, I have sinned and failed. I want to be born into Your Kingdom and serve You the rest of my life."

Belshazzar saw the handwriting on the wall and heard Daniel interpret God's message, "Thou art weighed in the balances, and art found wanting" (Daniel 5:27).

If there is any one message today that should be written across the United States and Canada and around the world, it is that our homes have sinned. They have failed, and are weighed in the balances and found wanting.

If God is speaking to your heart, repent now. Begin today to establish the Christian principles in your home that ought to be there. It is never too late to change, to be the kind of dad, mother, son or daughter that God wants you to be.

Put God first, and He will bless your home.

5

The Prodigal Mother

For the Son of man is come to seek and to save that
which was lost.   Luke 19:10

This story is a very pathetic one. It is about a young man and
how he struggled to save his family from the consequences of
sin.

The prophet Hosea was married to Gomer—a wicked, vile,
and evil woman. She was one who lived in whoredom. She
brought sin into the parsonage. This is her story. It is a picture
also of the people of Israel.

The scene of the story is Samaria, where Jeroboam, King of
Israel, lived. This city had become prosperous, and was so blessed
that money was flowing like wine, and people were full of
laughter and joy.

It is strange how some people who once loved God and served
Him were very cautious until they got good jobs, good homes,
and good automobiles. Then, they seemed to say, "Good-bye, God.
I don't need You any longer. I can find something to eat without
You. I can buy whatever I need now." And they forgot God.

So it was with the city of Samaria. Her people had become
very wicked. In their prosperity, with all of their luxuries, sin
had begun to crowd in upon them.

Ten years before this story happened, the prophet Amos had
stood up and prophesied, saying, "The Syrians are going to

encamp round about you. They are going to ride in with their great chariots and with their great horsemen. Repent of your evil ways and return unto the Lord." But they wouldn't listen to Amos any more than they listened to Hosea.

Now, you may read this sermon and say, "I know that man is right, but I am not going to do anything about it today." In the caverns of hell, you may remember this message.

Having had your opportunity, you will go into eternity without an excuse, you will have turned down the love of God, as the Samarians did. You will have turned down the message of the Lord.

My friend, any nation, any home, or any individual who turns down God's blessings finds out sooner or later that the wages of sin is death.

Gomer, who became Hosea's wife, must have been a charming young woman. As Hosea looked upon her, his love for her began to grow—even though he knew in his heart that he should not marry her. He knew she was not like him. Yet, his passion seemed to drive him on until one day they stood before an altar and were united in marriage.

Now, marriage can be the most heavenly thing in the world, or it can be hell on earth. Hosea soon found that it was far from heavenly to be married to an ungodly woman.

As the Holy Spirit moved upon Hosea to prophesy, he could hear the rumblings of the armies of the Syrians encamping about, just as Amos had predicted. The anointing of the Lord was mightily upon Hosea as he preached the Word of God.

But when Hosea came home at night his wife would look at him and say, "You have no time for me. You have no time to drink with me. You have no time to take me out to parties or to have social life at all. All I hear are these fairy tales and fables about God. I am getting sick and tired of hearing that we are going to have to repent and talk to God."

At night, after she had gone to bed, Hosea would walk the floors with a heavy heart. He thought he had married a companion who would help him carry his burdens and share the things he did, but he found this to be untrue. The distance between them began to grow and grow and grow.

(God revealed to this prophet later on that this was like Israel. God was married to Israel, but Israel wandered from God and broke His laws.)

Then, one day, the home of Hosea was blessed: A baby was born, and Hosea thought, "Surely, now Gomer and I will be truly bound together; this child will take my heart strings and Gomer's heart strings and pull them together and tie our two hearts into one united effort. But no sooner had the baby started toddling around through the house than the wife of this great prophet came to him and said, "I don't like this kind of life. I like the bright lights, and I want the sins and the pleasures of the world."

People whispered pretty things in her ear. "You are too young to be tied down to a serious, sober preacher," they said. "You are too young to be tied down to those old beliefs that you can't go out and have a good time. Eat, drink, and be merry, for tomorrow you may die. Some day you will be old and won't be able to have a good time. Then you can serve the Lord." (Isn't this just the way the devil talks to people God is dealing with?)

Gomer made her decision—and out into sin she went.

The distance between Hosea and his wife continued to grow. Another baby was born into the home, and Hosea named it "Unloved," because he had become suspicious that this child was not his own, but illegitimate.

As time rolled on, a third child was born and Hosea named it, "No Kin of Mine." His heart was heavy. And all the time the gulf between him and his wife grew greater.

One night he came home and walked into the nursery where the three little children were. One of them handed him a message.

He looked at it and read, "I am leaving. Don't search for me, because someone else has promised me happiness. Someone else has promised me pleasures and a good time. Don't come after me, for I am gone."

It was signed by Gomer, the mother of three children, the wife of a minister. She was gone—out into a life of sin and misery. Yes, gone!

That night the prophet Hosea knelt down beside the bed, put his arms around the three little children, and prayed. And he ended his prayer by saying, "Lord, bless Mother, wherever she is, and send her back home. Amen." Then he got up and slipped the children into bed. They were so young, they didn't understand, and soon they were asleep. But Hosea walked the floor. He paced from one room to another. He walked in and looked at the curly locks of his little girl. He looked at her lips. She didn't look like him, but like her mother. Hosea cried. He prayed. And then he called out in the darkness, "Gomer, please come back to us!"

It was during this trying hour that the Spirit of the Lord came upon the prophet and said, "This is like Israel, my people, that I was married to, the one I loved, the one I had bestowed my blessings upon and had brought close to my bosom—Israel, the one who was a companion to God."

Israel had wandered far from God, and the sins of her people stood between them and God. And God revealed to Hosea the terrible plague of sin, the load and burden that sin brought, the things that come into people's lives because of their sins. Here, we get the meaning of the story, an explanation of sin: The true meaning of sin is the broken relationship between man and his God.

Hosea also realized something else which made him think. Gomer was already a prodigal wife, even before she wrote the note and left home. Her heart was not filled with the things of God; her heart was not dedicated to her husband and her family.

She loved someone else, and even if she had stayed at home she would still have been a prodigal in her heart.

There were two boys in the Bible to whom Jesus referred, a prodigal son and an elder son, who stayed home. When the prodigal son returned, the elder one would have nothing to do with him. "I have been home all the time," he said, "and my dad has never killed a fatted lamb, a sheep or calf for me; he never made a great feast for my friends." Now, that elder son was just as much a prodigal as his brother, because he had hatred in his heart. He was jealous. He didn't want to see his brother come home.

As for Hosea, it was not a housekeeper he wanted; he could go out and hire a housekeeper. He didn't need someone to wash, iron and scrub. That is the trouble with many homes today. Homes should not be built upon washing, ironing, and scrubbing, but upon love. America needs the love of God in the hearts of the mothers and dads, so the children can be brought up in the fear of the Lord.

Hosea began to realize that God's people had left the fold and gone astray. They had not done the things they should have done.

In the New Testament, Matthew tells us that Jesus looked over Jerusalem and wept. He said, "How often would I have gathered thy children together . . . and ye would not" (Matthew 23:37)! Oh, how Jesus loved, and what compassion He had! Although the people of Jerusalem had failed God, He wanted them to come back. He urged them to repent, but they would not!

Yes, the story of Gomer is a terrible one, but it is also wonderful, for one day someone came by and said to Hosea, "You know what? I saw Gomer today."

"Where was she?" asked the prophet.

He learned that the man who had made her all those false promises had sold her into white slavery. She was a harlot. She had no freedom. She was in chains, and living in the lowest depths of corruption and sin.

"Now, surely, Hosea, you will get a divorce and let her go. You will have nothing to do with her any longer." This was the advice of a friend. But Hosea thought for a moment and then said, "Maybe, and maybe not."

I can assure you, there are people of all kinds, in all walks of life, to whom the devil has made a lot of promises he didn't fulfill. He has said, "You will have a good time and you will be happy." But you know what has happened? Many have ended up as alcoholics. Many have ended up with broken homes or with sick bodies. Many have ended up with tormented minds and guilty consciences.

The devil may tell you that you will have a good time, that he will give you freedom and the things you want. Yes, the devil makes many promises he will never fulfill, and sooner or later, if you listen to him, you will find yourself bound and chained and sold as a tool of sin because you have wandered from God.

I don't care in what state you may be, there is a God who still loves you. No matter where Gomer went or what she did, Hosea loved her. She was his wife and the mother of his children. Although those children may have been born out of wedlock, his heart was still filled with love.

Do you realize that God looks upon all of us as illegitimate? We were not born the way God planned, with the fellowship of the Lord. We were born and shaped in iniquity and sin. Every one of us is illegitimate, because our father is the devil. But Jesus Christ came and died on Calvary, and God still loves us, just as Hosea loved Gomer.

That night, as the sun began to sink in the west, Hosea started to the door and the three children followed him. "Where are you going, Daddy, and when will you be back?" they asked. He took them by their hands then patted them on their heads and said, "Children, Daddy is going to bring your mother home tonight."

Then Hosea went alone into the night. He didn't go to a house of honor, but to one of ill repute, and for fifteen pieces of silver and a parcel and a half of barley he purchased Gomer's freedom. "Loose that chain," he said. "This is my love. Loose the chain and let her go free." He then took the hand of this piece of human wreckage. She had sunk into the lowest depths of sin, but she was the one Hosea loved.

Oh, how many times the Holy Spirit has come, through the shed blood of the Lord, and has said, "Loose the chain, for Christ has purchased this one. This one is His own." No matter how low in sin we may go, no matter how far from Him we may stray, God is still with us.

The psalmist has said, "If I ascend up into heaven, thou art there: if I make my bed in hell, behold, thou art there" (Psalms 139:8). God is everywhere, and God's Spirit is searching after **you** today!

You may have made a complete wreck of things. You may be behind prison bars. Disease may wrack your mind and your body. Your family may have turned you out. But, don't forget, Jesus still loves you, like Hosea loved Gomer.

Hosea led Gomer back home to her three little children. The Bible doesn't tell us whether or not she left again. I hope she believed the Scriptures in the Old Testament: ". . . Though your sins be as scarlet, they shall be as white as snow; though they be red like crimson, they shall be as wool" (Isaiah 1:18).

Not too long ago, a young man came to see me. He had been drinking. He was under a load of sin. He fell across the altar and said, "I have lost my job, my home, my wife and my children." Then he cried, "Oh, God, cleanse me and save me today."

Instead of praying that day—as I usually do in such cases—I knelt there by him, laid my hand upon his shoulder and lifted my other hand as I sang the old hymn:

> There is a fountain, filled with blood,
> Drawn from Immanuel's veins;
> And sinners plunged beneath that flood,
> Lose all their guilty stains.

My friend, God applied the blood to that boy's heart. He saved his soul. Today he has a home, a job, and—most important of all —he has the priceless gift of salvation.

God wants to bring all of us back to the fold. Right now He is saying to the old slave master who has people bound in lives of sin, "Loose them and let them go free. I have paid the price. I have redeemed them at Calvary."

"For God so loved the world, that he gave his only begotten Son, that whosoever believeth in him should not perish, but have everlasting life" (John 3:16).

That promise is for you, wherever you are. You may be a prodigal. If so, you are headed for destruction.

God is calling you Home. Will you listen to that call and accept Him into your heart and life—TODAY?

6

The Gift of Helps

*And whether one member suffer, all the members
suffer with it; or one member be honoured, all the
members rejoice with it.*   1 Corinthians 12:26

If we want to live effective Christian lives, each of us must try to
find his or her own special place in the Kingdom.

In his first letter to the Corinthian church, Paul compares the
Body of Christ to the physical—the human body.

The physical body is made up of many different members, he
points out. There are the eye, the ear, the hand, the tongue, the
foot; and each of these individual members is a most important
part of the whole body. The eye is created for seeing. This, the
hand cannot do. The foot's responsibility is walking. The tongue
is supposed to talk—not walk, the ear, to hear. So, each member
of the physical body has a very definite and important task to
perform for the good of the whole. And any one part, regardless
of size, is just as important to the body as the others. So, the foot
shall not say, "Because I am not the hand, I am not of the body."
Likewise, "if the whole body were an eye, where were the hearing?" And "if the whole were hearing, where were the smelling"
(1 Corinthians 12:15, 17)?

There must be no division in the body. Each member should
have care and concern for the others. "And whether one member
suffer, all the members suffer with it." On the other hand, if "one
member be honoured, all the members rejoice with it."

In other words, if I slam the car door on my hand my brain is certainly going to know about it. My whole arm is going to know about it. Even my heart will know about it, because the pulsation of that organ will be a little bit different. And my mouth will undoubtedly fly open as I cry out with pain!

So, as each member is an integral part of the whole body, it is thus with all the believers that make up the Body of Christ. Each member is important, and there must be no division or separation. In this Body, God has placed some apostles, some prophets, some teachers, "after that miracles, then gifts of healings, helps, governments, diversities of tongues." But "are all apostles? are all prophets? are all teachers? are all workers of miracles? Have all the gifts of healing? do all speak with tongues? do all interpret? But covet earnestly the best gifts: and yet shew I unto you a more excellent way" (1 Corinthians 12:28–31).

Although each gift has different manifestations and administrations, all are necessary to the whole Body. This sermon concerns the Gift of Helps!

This gift is one which people often do not want to acknowledge or accept. Most of us would prefer to be in the positions of leadership or prominence—as an apostle, a prophet, or one who speaks in tongues. We would rather work miracles or do something else, rather than simply being a helper. I don't hear many people in the prayer room of my church saying, "Lord, give me the gift of 'helps,' let me be a helper in the Kingdom of God." Nevertheless, although not many pray to be helpers, I want to impress on you that those who help are just as important as any who stand in prominent places.

You will remember the account in the Old Testament (Exodus, chapter 17) of the battle between the Children of Israel and Amalek. Moses, accompanied by Aaron and Hur, went to "stand on the top of the hill with the rod of God in his hand" as Joshua led the fight. As long as Moses held up his hands, the Israelites defeated the enemy on all sides. However, Moses was a human being as well as an instrument of God; and he got tired.

If you have ever held your arms up in the air for very long, you know that the pain finally becomes unbearable. So, Moses' arms became too painful for him to hold up in his own strength. The pain was too great, the fatigue too much, and he lowered his arms. Now, as long as Moses held his hands in the air, God was with him, but when he lowered his hands, the enemy began to take over.

Then what happened? Two men—not the one whom God had called out as the leader (Moses), not the one who was called to lead the army, fight the war, and win the victory (Joshua)—but two other men came to be Moses' helpers. They set him on a rock. One of them got under one arm and said, "You must hold up your arms, Moses, but you are so weak that you can't do it any longer. So, I am going to help you." Up went one hand! Then the other helper got under the other arm and both hands were up in the air!

Thank God for people who have the gift of "helps," who know where they have been called to work and what they have been called to do.

YOUR PLACE

Is your place a small place?
Tend it with care;—
He set you there.

Is your place a large place?
Guard it with care!—
He set you there.

Whate'er your place, it is
Not yours alone, but His
Who set you there.

—JOHN OXENHAM

Many people would not have taken that task of holding up Moses' arms, because Moses got the credit for winning the war, even though it was not really he who won it. Actually, God won the victory that day. Moses was only the instrument in God's hands.

This same principle holds true in the salvation of individuals. Few were ever saved through the efforts of one person alone. When people come to the altar, dedicate their lives to Christ, and are born into the Kingdom of God, I get to pray with them and rejoice at the time. But back of it all perhaps there is an old-fashioned praying mother who has been pleading for ten, twenty, thirty years, or even more for that son or daughter to get right with God. Sometimes it is the children who have prayed for their parents. Perhaps it was a seed planted years ago by some faithful Sunday-school teacher who stood in the classroom and taught that boy or girl the things of God. I just happened to come along at harvesttime. Someone else has done the "helping," but I have the privilege of rejoicing in the results. It is a wonderful privilege to pray with that person, but in the background there usually is someone who has believed, prayed, and given of himself or herself—someone with the gift of "helps."

In Chapter 9 of Acts is the story of Saul, later known as Paul, a dedicated missionary of the Gospel. At first, of course, he was not a believer. He certainly was not dedicated to the Kingdom of God, though he practiced all of the religious forms and rituals. As an educated leader of his religion, Saul thought it was his duty to destroy the disciples and leaders of this new faith.

With the great outpouring of the Spirit on the Day of Pentecost, God had given the Christians the commission to go into all the world and preach the Gospel unto every creature. But they had sat in Jerusalem praising the Lord for the blessings they had. With the persecution which God allowed to fall on it, however, the Church suddenly began to flee for its life. As the disciples fled from city to city they told about their faith, and thus became missionaries because of their persecution. And Saul went out to do God a favor by killing Christians.

At this time, Stephen, a man of much faith who believed in God and was full of the Holy Ghost, was witnessing for Christ and proclaiming the Gospel. To silence him, members of the synagogue bribed some men to testify that Stephen had blasphemed against Moses and God. As was the custom in such cases, they then took Stephen outside the city walls to stone him to death. Now Saul, in his zeal to destroy the Christians, was one of those who consented to this mockery of justice, and he was present at the stoning.

But, in all of this, Stephen became God's helper in bringing about the salvation of an unbeliever. How did he do it? He prayed, as the rocks began to hit him, "Lord Jesus, receive my spirit." Then he kneeled down and cried out, "Lord, lay not this sin to their charge."

He knew that it was the enemy, the devil, in their hearts that caused them to do what they did. He knew that each of them had a soul, and he wanted to see their souls saved. Think of it: Although they were casting stones at him, killing him, he still wanted them to be saved! He didn't want this act to be put on their record before the Lord.

Thus, by praying for those who were stoning him, Stephen became a helper in the salvation of Saul of Tarsus.

Saul's zeal to destroy Jesus' followers continued, and he obtained a decree from the synagogue leaders to pursue the Christians into Damascus, where some had fled. His orders were to bring them back to Jerusalem, where they could be tried and thrown into prison or killed. Although he was very religious, Saul knew nothing of the salvation of the Lord; he thought he was doing God a favor. He was going to wipe out these believers because he feared they would destroy the old religion's form and ritual—perhaps even the temple, because their good news was spreading rapidly.

It was on the road to Damascus that God Almighty confronted Saul and answered the prayer of His helper, Stephen. As Saul traveled along, God reached out of the portals of Glory, through the power of the Holy Ghost, and tapped him right on the head.

Blinded by a great light, Saul fell to the ground; and a voice said, "It is hard for thee to kick against the pricks." (This referred to the sharp stick by which donkeys were prodded when they got stubborn and refused to move.)

Saul asked, "Who art thou, Lord?"

And the reply came, "I am Jesus whom thou persecutest" (Acts 9:5).

When Saul opened his eyes, he was blind. He had to be led by his men into the city, not as a great man, with orders from the temple; not as a man who commanded soldiers, going to arrest the Christians; but as a sightless man who was now ready to listen to God. So he was led into Damascus, where one by the name of Ananias went in and laid hands upon him and prayed for him, that he might receive the Holy Ghost and his sight. At once, Saul's sight was restored, and he was filled with the Holy Ghost.

Saul was a learned man, a great man of his day. So when news got around that he had been blinded but now could see, and that he claimed to be a believer, fear came to the hearts of the Christians. They were sure that he was only making a profession of faith so that he might get in among them, find out who they were and then have them all arrested.

When Saul returned to Jerusalem, Barnabas was the only one who said, "He has really been born again." While the others were afraid because of the previous persecutions, Barnabas said,

"He has had a real experience; we must have fellowship with him." Here was another helper!

Now Paul began preaching Christ with all of the vigor and earnestness he had formerly used against the Christians. And every time he preached he made more enemies among the Jews. Finally, his enemies became so angry that they said, "We have to get Paul." The word went out: "Get Paul! He has blasphemed God. We are going to kill him."

Now, Paul was being warred against on the very same grounds on which he used to war against others. He had to escape, but the city gates were guarded and he was unable to get out. Finally, his friends came to his rescue. They put him in a basket, tied a rope to it, and lowered him over the city wall as night. They, too, possessed the gift of "helps."

Those believers knew that they might be caught helping Paul escape, but they were willing to take that chance. Little did they realize that they were saving a man who would become the world's greatest missionary, who would write most of the New Testament, under divine revelation of Almighty God. Little did they know that this man would establish the first church ever called Christian, the church at Antioch. Little did they understand the importance of their gift of "helps."

So, neither do you know how your help will be used. If you are that mother who has been reading the Bible and praying with your children, whose souls which have been entrusted to you, you may be the only helper those children will ever have who can lead them to know Jesus Christ.

There are invalids who say, "I wish I could go to a mission field." Other people would like to preach on television, "like Rex." And some want to be heads of departments, etc. But I want you to know that *everyone* is important—from the smallest child to the oldest man or woman. YOU are important! You may not get in the *Who's Who*. The world, as a whole, may never know you. But God knows you, and you are important to Him. Keep praying and believing, because you are part of the Kingdom of God, in whatever way you may be serving Him.

There are many ways you can be endued with this gift of "helps" to the Kingdom of God. By just living the Christian life, by being an example of Christ, by showing forth His love through your heart and life, you may be helping others to find Him.

Another gift of "helps" is through prayer. One of the most touching experiences I ever had was when a mother came to me with a little child who was completely paralyzed. The child was about ten years old, but her arms and legs were ever so small, and she was a complete invalid.

In my office, the mother held her child lovingly and said, "My baby was born this way and continues thus. Will you pray for me, that God will give me strength? And will you pray for my child?"

She was the only person in the world who could have held on to that little bundle. She couldn't let go, because God had entrusted her with that baby—she was its one help.

May God give you the help which only He can give, to carry your own burdens. And may He also give you the help to become a helper, and to express His love and care to this human race.

So often I have asked, "Why, Lord? Why would you thrust on me the responsibility for the Cathedral of Tomorrow, for Mackinac College, the TV ministry, the rallies, and all the rest? Lord, I am not capable, and I am not worthy."

Then I think of the thousands of people who are praying, the thousands who stand by with their gifts, the thousands who are believing God; and I say, "Thank you, Lord, that I have, not only You, but dedicated helpers, besides!"

Aren't you glad someone helped you to find Jesus Christ? If so, your duty now is to help others find Him. And all of us, as Christians, have the duty of strengthening and upholding the other members of the Body: for "whether . . . one member be honoured, all the members rejoice with it."

God help us to dedicate ourselves to being helpers, so that we can bring more and more souls to a saving knowledge of our Lord and Saviour, Jesus Christ!

7

What Are the Greater Things That Jesus Promised?

But when he saw the multitudes, he was moved with compassion on them, because they fainted, and were scattered abroad, as sheep having no shepherd. Then saith he unto his disciples, The harvest truly is plenteous, but the labourers are few; Pray ye therefore the Lord of the harvest, that he will send forth labourers into his harvest. Matthew 9:36–38

As we have seen, everyone who calls himself a Christian can find ways to become a helper in the Kingdom of God. There has never been a time in the history of the world when the opportunity to reach out with the Gospel has been so great as it is in this age.

On the other hand, there's never been a time when the attraction away from God and His Presence, to sin, has been greater.

This is a day when it is easy to have hatred, easy to have strife, easy to be worried, easy to sin. And yet, there's never been an age when the grace of God was not sufficient to meet the needs in people's lives.

As we look at our world and its exploding population, we find it took 5,830 years before we had one billion people on the face of the earth.

We multiplied so fast that the second billion arrived in the next 100 years.

The third billion arrived in only 33 years.

And in the next 10-year period, there will be another billion people on this planet.

The astounding fact is this: In 10 years as many new people will appear on the face of the earth as it once took 5,830 years to produce!

This means there are more people living and breathing right now than have lived and died from the time of Adam and Eve until today.

The challenge to Christians today is monumental—as great, I'm convinced, as that faced by any previous generation.

Jesus has promised, "He that believeth on me, the works that I do shall he do also; and greater works than these shall he do; because I go unto my Father" (John 14:12).

He also said, "But the Comforter, which is the Holy Ghost, whom the Father will send in my name, he shall teach you all things, and bring all things to your remembrance, whatsoever I have said unto you" (John 14:26).

In the Old Testament, God dealt with man. In the New Testament, Jesus dealt with man. And now in this Holy Ghost dispensation, the Holy Spirit deals with man to present Christ in His beauty and glory.

And yet, Jesus told his followers that they would do the works He did, and "greater works than these . . . because I go unto my Father."

What are the "greater works"?

Jesus opened blind eyes, unstopped deaf ears, made the lame to walk, even raised the dead—but these are not the "greater works."

The "greater work" is the salvation of souls. In fact, there is *no* greater work than helping a soul be born into the Kingdom of God.

We are not talking of Jesus and His deity.

I am old-fashioned enough to believe the Scripture that God so loved the world that He gave His Son; that Christ so loved the world that He was willing to come into it; and that He was born of the Virgin Mary—He had no earthly father.

He came to die, and He bore your sin and mine on his own body on the tree.

This work that Jesus performed at Calvary—only He, in His deity, could do that.

When Jesus said, "The works that I do shall he do also, and greater works than these . . . ," He was not referring to His work on the cross. He was speaking of His earthly ministry. You see, Jesus did not reach as many people with the Gospel in His lifetime as we speak to each Sunday over television.

The "greater work" is the salvation of many souls. If one soul is saved, it's a great work—and if it's your soul I know you'll agree with me. But if two souls are saved, that's a greater work.

In this generation in which we live, the "greater work" that Christ wants done is the bringing of great numbers of people into the Kingdom of God.

In this age, we have more souls to win, more opportunities to reach them, and better means of communicating the Gospel to a greater number of people in a shorter time than ever before.

Where does a spiritual awakening fit into the program of God in these days?

Let's look at Joel 2:23–26:

"Be glad then, ye children of Zion, and rejoice in the Lord your God: for he hath given you the former rain moderately, and he will cause to come down for you the rain, the former rain, and the latter rain in the first month.

"And the floors shall be full of wheat, and the fats shall overflow with wine and oil.

"And I will restore to you the years that the locust hath eaten, the cankerworm, and the caterpillar, and the palmerworm, my great army which I sent among you.

"And ye shall eat in plenty, and be satisfied, and praise the name of the Lord your God, that hath dealt wondrously with you: and my people shall never be ashamed."

Here we've read a reference to the former and latter rain. Let's look for a moment to the land where Jesus was speaking, the land of Palestine.

If you know anything about that land, you know there comes an early, or "former," rain in October and November. It comes to prepare the soil and nourish the seed.

During the winter months there are spasmodic showers. And then about April there come the latter rains in Palestine. These latter rains are followed by heat, and that is when it is harvest time.

We are now in the closing moments of this Holy Ghost dispensation. What are we to expect? What are we to prepare for? What are we to believe in?

The latter rain is not for the breaking up of the soil, nor for the planting of the seed, nor for the spasmodic showers and growth; the pouring out of God's Spirit in these days is for HARVEST-TIME!

Everything you and I do now ought to be in preparation for the harvest. All you have to do is lift up your eyes to see that already the fields are white!

The Bible says, "Pray ye therefore the Lord of the harvest, that he would send forth labourers into his harvest" (Luke 10:2).

I believe we are living on the threshold of the greatest spiritual harvest the world has ever seen.

In the first place, the need is here. There are more people living now than have lived since the beginning of time. Second, God's Word teaches that the wicked will wax worse and worse, deceiving and being deceived. And we see that on every hand.

But Paul said that when Christ comes back, He is coming for a Church without spot, wrinkle, and blemish (see Ephesians 5:27). But the Church is not without spot, wrinkle, or blemish. There must be a spiritual ingathering, an awakening, a shower to ready the harvest, and God's people must go into the field and gather the harvest in.

This is where I feel the Church is at this very hour.

If we'll look at Samson's life, we can see a story similar to the history of the Church. When the Spirit of the Lord came upon Samson, he had great strength and power. One time he picked up the gates of the city, walked out, and set them down on a hillside.

In a similar way, the Early Church had the outpouring of Pentecost, and God told them to go and witness in Jerusalem, Judea, and the uttermost parts of the earth. But they were so blessed that they just sat around Jerusalem and would not go out into all the world.

When persecution came upon the Church, though, they fanned out in every direction. And everywhere they went, they talked about the Lord.

This era of witnessing was the season of rain to plant the seed—to build the early New Testament Church and cause people to start growing in the grace and knowledge of the Lord. Like Samson, the Church was using the power it had received from God.

But one day, we find Samson bound and being led away.

In like manner, we find that the Early Church finally cooled down. They looked at other religions and began to take them in. And the churches became so pagan that there was no dividing line between Christians and pagans. The Church lost out.

While Samson was being led away, a great anointing came upon him. The Spirit of the Lord gave him power, and he broke asunder his bonds and killed 1,000 Philistines with the jawbone of a donkey!

Likewise, we find that the Church broke loose from its paganism, and began to thrust itself throughout the world again with light, vibrancy, and power.

Samson made a fatal mistake; he went back and laid his head on the lap of Delilah. He revealed his secret to her, and she had his hair cut off.

In like manner, the Church became worldly. It no longer shunned or denounced sin. To become a member of the Church and still tolerate sin became popular.

Do you realize that we have churches right now where you could be the biggest gambler in town, the biggest alcoholic, or be married three or four times, and still be a member?

We have churches where they gamble in the basements. They don't have their Sunday night service, but they have their smoking club and their juke box, and run dances on Sunday night in the basement of the church.

I do not believe the Church should bring in sin; it should put sin out. We're not angels, but I tell you we can lift up a standard. And people will be interested if we do.

And what happened when Samson laid his head in the lap of Delilah, told his secret, and had his hair cut off? The first thing they did was to take him and put out his eyes.

Like Samson, the Church lost its vision.

Do you know that the United States alone has the financial ability and the church membership to be able to send missionaries and evangelize the whole world? But we haven't done it.

At the end of World War II, Douglas MacArthur asked for missionaries to go to all the islands of the sea. He knew they needed God. He knew they needed the Gospel. But we didn't have the missionaries to send.

Instead, we held on to our own convenience and our luxury— and we let the world go to hell. We have laid our head in the lap of the world and lost, first of all, our vision to go into all the world and preach the Gospel.

Samson not only had his eyes gouged out; he was hooked up to a grist mill where he took the part of a donkey. Around, and around he went.

I've seen church machinery and denominations going in circles, too. They'll call committee meetings, fill out papers, draw up plans—and never reach one soul for Jesus Christ.

Let's face up. Let's examine ourselves and our times and realize what's happening in these closing days.

One day, Samson was grinding at the mill. His hair had grown back. And the Philistines decided to take him into the great arena, to make a mockery of him. You know the story: As the crowd jeered, Samson prayed for his strength to be restored.

And now we see him standing between the pillars of the temple as he cries out, "O Lord God . . . strengthen me . . ." (Judges 16:28).

This is the hour I believe the Church is in right now. It is waiting for the restoration of power once again.

And the Bible says Samson pulled the pillars of that great temple and there was a mighty crash. Samson died a champion. He killed more of the enemy that day than he did in his whole lifetime.

I believe right now we can say, "God, restore Your power unto Your people," and under His anointing we can see more people brought into the harvest in this one generation than have been brought to God from Adam and Eve until now!

What causes me to walk the floors till the wee hours of the morning, to mortgage everything I've got to get on another TV station is this: I believe time is running out.

NOW is the time to say, "Lord, restore!"

How are we going to take on the challenge of this world with its exploding population?

We can't do it the way we were doing 20 years ago. At that time, I had travelled for 12 years throughout America with my parents, my brother, and my sisters. And then one day, the Lord began to show me a new direction.

I told my family, "You go ahead in evangelism. I'm staying in Akron." I stayed there with $65 in my pocket. I had no church members, no church.

We called a few people together and incorporated under the laws of Ohio. And I told them, "We're going to build a large church. We're going to take the church service in its simplicity, and the old-fashioned Gospel, and, through television, take them into every state in the Union.

There wasn't any Bishop Sheen, Billy Graham or Oral Roberts on TV then—no ministers were using TV in those days. But the Lord let me see this great world with its growing need. I saw that the people weren't in their churches, and that the way to reach them was to go where they were, through the medium of television.

As I'd fly across America and look down at the cities, the farming communities, and the villages, I'd say to myself, "There's a potential pulpit next Sunday—through TV." And that thought still goes through my mind today every time I fly over the land.

God has helped me in some wonderful way with His Spirit and His anointing. And now, it is my privilege to participate in God's "greater works": on Sundays, I preach, on hundreds of stations, to thousands of viewers across the country.

8

There Are No Silent Christians

. . . ye should earnestly contend for the faith which
was once delivered unto the saints.   Jude 3

In the preceding chapter we talked about the "greatest work"—
saving souls. Now, if we are to perform that work it is clear that
we have to be ready to stand up and speak out for what we
believe. And when we do that, we might naturally expect the
support of our fellow Christians.

Humanity is strange, however, and people who do good are
often hindered in every possible way—even by the so-called "good
people."

A good example is in the life of Jesus Himself. He lived a lonely
life. He bore the sins of the world in death, yet while He was
living the scribes, Pharisees, priests, and the religious world
would have nothing to do with Him. And in the end He was
forsaken, even by His own disciples. Today we know that this
One rejected of men was the Chief Cornerstone. He is the salvation of the human race, just as He was then—the Deliverer of the
world. He is our Lord, and our Saviour; our Sacrifice for sin and
uncleanness; our soon coming King, and He is building for us
mansions on the hillsides of glory.

Yes, we love Him now, but He was never appreciated while He
was here. Life is like that; those who have contributed most to
the Kingdom of God have been stoned and mocked, crucified and

slain, derided and scoffed at. Peter, who preached the memorable sermon on Pentecost, was crucified upside down because he was a just man.

I could come to town with a circus, a nightclub, a bar, or a dance hall, and men of reputation and wealth—businessmen— would compliment me, and my integrity would be unquestioned. A lot of church members would patronize my business. In all likelihood, not one feeble preacher would lift a voice against anything that I did. I can't understand the religious world today. We want to conquer sin, yet we have it on every street corner in every city today. But isn't it a strange thing that where good deeds are done, righteous people rise up to fight the work of the Holy Ghost?

In John 9 we read about a man who was born blind. He sat by the side of the road, begging. Jesus made a little ball of clay, anointed his eyes, and told him to wash in the pool of Siloam and he would see. After this man went to the pool and found he could see just like other men, he was thrilled.

The neighbors gathered and some said, "This is he," while others said, "He *resembles* him." It was difficult for them to believe that here stood the blind man who had sat by the wayside and begged. So they asked him, and he said, "I am he." There is nothing like a living testimony. It is good to talk about Moses and Abraham, Isaac and Jacob, Peter and Paul, James and John; but how much better it is to see people step up and say, "I am a Christian" by their actions as well as by their words. How good it is to be a living testimony to the power of God!

Following this miracle, the authorities called the beggar in and said, "Now listen, you can't give credit to Jesus. You have to give credit to the synagogue." There is a lot of that today. You cannot give credit to God, you must give credit to the church, the denomination, or some individual. This is all wrong. God merits the honor and the glory. Jesus deserves the praise for that which He has done. Though it is through the operation of the nine spiritual gifts, it is still the Lord that sends the Holy Ghost. And when the Holy Ghost comes, He brings the things of God to life.

In the synagogue the former blind man was questioned by the Jews. They would not believe his testimony, so they sent for his parents, and they, too, were questioned. Something had happened to their son, it was apparent, and he did not hesitate to tell them about it. But nothing had happened to the parents, who should have been overjoyed. Do you know why they did not have a word of witness? Because nothing had happened to them personally. It matters not how much you keep company with religious people, how much you attend church, or how close to God your wife or children draw, if you do not know God yourself, you will not have a testimony. It takes personal experience. We need an inward work in our lives as individuals.

The parents feared the rulers of the synagogue. They didn't wish to be thrown out, or to be ridiculed, so they said, "We know that this is our son, and that he was born blind: But by what means he now seeth, we know not, . . . he is of age; ask him: he shall speak for himself" (John 9:20, 21).

There are people like that today. They can talk about healing, but they have never been healed. They can talk about salvation, but they know not when they were saved, how they were saved, who saved them, or what they were saved from. Their lives have not changed. They will tell you about the Lord, but when it is all boiled down what have they got in their lives to prove that God has done a real work for them personally?

This young men had been healed, and he could not be silent. They finally threw him out of the synagogue. You may be treated likewise. You may be thrown out of your community church, but just remember, the Lord will always pick you up, just as Jesus came along and picked up the man whose sight had been restored.

Not long ago I was flying about nine thousand feet in the air. Beside me was seated a man with whom I had flown to Chicago, a businessman in my community. We got to talking about God, and I told him how happy I was because I was a Christian. He said, "Well, I am, too. I always like to take Christ with me in my business. No matter where I am I bow my head and return thanks. I try to do the things I ought to do everywhere I go. In New York, Chicago, Philadelphia or wherever, I try to witness for the Lord." Then he looked at me and said, "Rex, there are no silent Christians."

When I heard that, something happened in my heart. There was a magnificent witness there. It is true: There ARE no silent Christians. The only people who have a right to call themselves Christians are those whose hands are dedicated to God; whose feet are dedicated to God; whose eyes are dedicated to God; whose entire life is dedicated to God and who are being used by God in His service. They are the only Christians.

Then I began to think. "Listen to that noise. These huge motors make a tremendous noise. Now if that noise would stop and all became silent, I would make some noise." Why? Because I would be alarmed: If the motors had stopped making a noise, they would have been dead.

Your automobile makes a noise as the motor vibrates. When that motor stops, you know something is wrong: Either the ignition has been turned off or the motor is defective or you are out of gas. Silence means that the motor is dead; and silence in a person who names the name of Jesus means that that one is dead.

Peter and John went down to the temple one day, to pray. And they found a lame man sitting by the wayside. When the man asked them for money, Peter said, "Silver and gold have I none; but such as I have give I thee: In the name of Jesus

Christ of Nazareth rise up and walk" (Acts 3:6). The man was
so grateful that he went over to the synagogue and worshipped
and praised God.

Too many people are silent about their Christianity. It is so
private and precious and sacred to them that it doesn't affect
the world at all. What was the man healed for? What did the
power of God come through that man for? To make him well,
yes, but more. You know what happened? Limbs that were one
time crippled began to leap, and the man began to praise God.

The excitement attracted a great crowd. They pressed into
Solomon's porch, and thank God that Peter and John knew what
to do when they got a crowd. They didn't stand around and talk
about the limbs that were healed. No! They didn't talk about
how long this man had been a cripple. No! "Ye men of Israel,
why marvel ye at this?" Peter asked. "Or why look ye so earnestly
on us, as though by our own power or holiness we had made
this man to walk? The God of Abraham, and of Isaac, and of
Jacob, the God of our fathers, hath glorified his Son Jesus; . . .
And his name through faith in his name hath made this man
strong" (Acts 3:12, 13, 16). Five thousand people were saved
that day because someone was not silent about what God had
done.

If all of us would tell how God has saved us from eternal hell
and healed us from our afflictions, how He has blessed us and
provided for us, the glory of God could be made manifest in
countless lives. On the other hand, if you are one of those who
go to church and worship God and then go out, leaving Jesus
Christ behind, and go on about their work just as before, you
are becoming a silent Christian. This is a dangerous sign, because
there are no silent Christians.

Oh, but you say, "I know of a man who prayed three times a
day. They cautioned him that if he didn't stop his praying they
would throw him into the lion's den, but he just went ahead

as before, praying to his God, and he didn't make a big scene about it. He was silent." Yes, but he went into the lion's den, my friend. Let me tell you that silent night Daniel spent in that den was the most open, outward confession that he had ever given.

A lot of folks can testify and sing and shout, but I wonder, can the world see God in your life while you're in a lion's den? How many onlookers can see the peace and the calm with which you face the battles of life? Silent Christians? There are no silent Christians!

The night Daniel spent in the lion's den didn't find him moaning and groaning and trying to climb out. Was he frustrated, worried, discouraged, and blue? No! Daniel rested his case in the arms of the Lord. And the Lord brought him out all right.

Daniel's actions that night spoke his testimony and caused more faith to be placed in the living God than anything he had ever done in all of his life. If you want others to have faith in the God you serve, then act like a Christian. You don't have to tell everyone that you are a Christian and that you attend services regularly. No! You just walk and talk and look as a Christian should and soon someone will want to know if you go to church and where. Then tell him.

There is a time to shout. That time is when you are saved— when you are healed. Then the crowd will gather. It would have been quite the opposite if the man who was born lame had just sat there and shouted, "Jesus can heal, Jesus can heal, folks."

It would have been a different testimony. There would never have been five thousand on Solomon's porch. It took more than talk. It took action, too.

There are no silent Christians. If you are a Christian, your life is influencing someone to live closer to Jesus or to seek the face of the Lord. Your life is influencing someone in need if you are a Christian.

Christ meets the needs of the world. If you will do as God

directs, you will be healed. If you want your loved ones saved, take them to church. Go where God is, and where God's people are. In the first chapter of this book we talked about Naaman, who was a leper. A little maid had been captured and taken down into bondage. Since she was in a foreign land she thought the best thing for her to do was never to mention her God. Right? No! One day she went to her mistress and told her there was a God in Israel that would heal her husband if he would only go to see the Prophet Elisha.

That little maid, whose life didn't mean very much by the world's standards, caused the captain of the people, their great leader, to be healed of leprosy because she testified. Would you have thought her a follower of God if she had gone to Syria, to the household of Naaman, who was dying of leprosy, and remained silent, even though she knew of a God who could heal him? Would she have been a follower of God had she kept her mouth closed? No, she had to speak out. Why are any of us saved? To tell others the story of Jesus. You will have eternal life someday, but *today* is the day of salvation. *Today* is the time to work for Jesus.

It's time to get alarmed if the motors quit. That plane I mentioned would have caused me to get excited if the motors had suddenly become silent. How many of us get alarmed if our motors quit, spiritually speaking, and our lives stop telling for Jesus? Our voices no longer tell the story. Our hands quit working. Our eyes quit seeing the beauties of the Lord. Our souls quit absorbing God's Word and His blessings. How many of us get as alarmed as we would if the motors stopped in the air? If our own motors stop, it is time for us to get alarmed, for it is a dangerous situation.

There are no silent Christians. Christ is the Door, but you and I are the doorkeepers. You and I can invite people to come into the Kingdom of God or keep people out. Beside that Door are the born-again Christians, either ready to open it to bring in lost souls or standing there with folded arms doing nothing. Christ wants a revival. Christ wants people to come into the Kingdom. You and I are the doorkeepers, the bearers of that Light to the earth. The only light the world may see is the Light of Christ that shines through you and me.

9

Putting First Things First

Now it came to pass, as they went, that he entered into a certain village: and a certain woman named Martha received him into her house. And she had a sister called Mary, which also sat at Jesus' feet, and heard his word. But Martha was cumbered about much serving, and came to him, and said, Lord, dost Thou not care that my sister hath left me to serve alone? bid her therefore that she help me. And Jesus answered and said unto her, Martha, Martha, thou art careful and troubled about many things: But one thing is needful; and Mary hath chosen that good part, which shall not be taken away from her.

Luke 10:38–42

Suddenly, unannounced, unexpected, from the City of Jerusalem came a little group of men—Jesus and His disciples. They traveled over the Mount of Olives, down the little pathway on the other side, and—just beyond the Mount of Olives—to Bethany.

This little village was the home of some of Jesus' most personal and intimate friends—Mary, Martha and Lazarus, whom He loved dearly. Now, by the inference of the Scripture, Martha was the head of the house, and ruled things. So as they came down the hill she invited them, and they all went in.

With twelve hungry men, plus the Master, Martha had to get

busy, and quickly. But Mary followed Jesus into what we might call the living room, and, as the custom was in those days, she got a towel and wiped the dust from His feet. Then Jesus began to talk, and Mary sat there, listening. She wasn't going to leave or rush about; she wasn't going to miss hearing what He was saying. It was a message about God and eternal life, and the spiritual food she was receiving made her forget all about dinner.

But this wasn't true with Martha. I imagine Martha was concerned about sufficient food and the general preparations. She had not known they were coming. So, she was real busy getting everything done. She was worried and disturbed, and finally she thought, "Why doesn't my sister come and help me?" Then she began to get mad; she was worried because she wanted to fix a good dinner, and she wanted everything to go well. These were special people in her home. So, she ran in, looked at Jesus and said, "Master, don't you care? Make my sister get up from there and come in here and help me." Although Jesus loved Martha, He rebuked her, saying, ". . . thou art careful and troubled about many things. . . ."

Why did Jesus rebuke Martha? Not because she wasn't a good woman. She was a good woman! You know people by what they do, not by what they say. Reputation is what people say you are; character is what God knows you are, and there is a big difference. Yes, Martha was a good woman; she was one who would serve. I imagine she was the kind who would come over and sit with you when you were sick; I imagine she was the kind who would share what she had if you were out of food and had no work. She would be one who would come into your home and try to help when you were in trouble. If there was work to be done at the church, she would be there. She was that kind of woman. Jesus did not rebuke her because she was not a good woman, because she was!

And Jesus did not rebuke her because she didn't love Him;

she did! Didn't she open her door and invite Him in? Wasn't He
her friend? Although Jesus was criticized in the temple and in
the synagogue by the priests, the elders, the rabbis and all the
rest, she still opened her door. I am sure her own neighbors
said, "Why do you want to associate with Him; don't you know
He is despised up at the place of worship? They are going to
count you one of them, because 'birds of a feather flock
together.'" But she loved Him enough that she opened her
home to Him, just the same. No, Jesus did not rebuke her because
she did not love Him. She was a Christian—she was a believer!

Jesus did not rebuke her because she was industrious; He
knew dinner had to be fixed. He knows also that you have to go
to work. He knows all of the burden you carry, Mother, in
washing and scrubbing those little youngsters, getting their
clothes ready, getting them off to school, cooking the meals, and
everything else. Jesus knows all about this. He knows about
your business, Dad, and the problems you face every day.
He knows they must be taken care of. So, Jesus did not rebuke Martha because she was in a hurry trying to get dinner
fixed. He rebuked her for two things: "Thou are careful and
troubled. . . ."

Christian people should have peace. Any time we don't have
peace, we have placed the lesser things first and the first things
second. The Bible tells us, "Thou wilt keep him in perfect peace,
whose mind is stayed on thee" (Isaiah 26:3). This doesn't say
that we won't have conflicts. It doesn't say that we won't have
to work. But when we go to work, we can take Jesus with us.
And when we run up against a wall and can't go through, when
we don't know what to do, we can talk to Jesus about it. And
when there are perplexing things—when company drops in and
dinner is not ready, for instance—we still can have peace. With
the Lord first, these other things will be taken care of.

Jesus rebuked her. He said, "Martha, Martha thou art careful and troubled about many things." One thing is needful: "But seek ye first the kingdom of God, and his righteousness; and all these things shall be added unto you" (Matthew 6:33). Mary sought fellowship with Jesus first. She knew that sooner or later He would get hungry, that she would get hungry, and then they would get dinner. But she wasn't going to sacrifice her fellowship with Him. Instead, she put it above all else.

Martha sought the dinner first. She thought she could get her fellowship later. But you'll be so anxious and so troubled, you will never have the fellowship unless you take it first; and you are not nearly so troubled and anxious if you have had that fellowship. Oh, this is so simple, but it is so true. And Jesus rebuked one He loved because she was troubled and anxious.

If life was complicated two thousand years ago when Jesus was here, how much more complicated it is today! God, help us, we have so much more about which to be troubled! So much more to do! So many more things that press in upon us! For it seems that the more we have, the more we have to worry about. Isn't that true? Jesus rebuked Martha because she was a slave to things; she was a slave to her work. We are not to be slaves to anything, but instead, free people in Jesus Christ.

This is the point I want you to consider and think upon: Are you a slave? ARE YOU A SLAVE? Well, think of your life for a moment! If you are so busy with your work, so busy with your business, so busy with your housekeeping, so busy with everything else that you have no time to fellowship with Jesus or to read your Bible or to pray or to go to church or to do Christian service; if you are so busy that you can do nothing to win souls or help with God's work, then you are a slave to "things." And Jesus rebukes that. We should be free people, and then we should joyfully take the tasks which are in our hands, because it is a joy to work, if we work in the name of the Lord. ". . . whatsoever ye do, do all to the glory of God" (1 Corinthians 10:31).

There is great danger in becoming a slave today. Even the minister can't be just a pastor to preach sermons and study God's Word anymore. You don't have any idea of the entailment and the business involvement and all else that goes on in connection with the Cathedral of Tomorrow, with the television, the out-of-town meetings, and everything that has to be done. It is just one thing after another, so that Rex Humbard, or any other minister—if he is not careful—can become a slave to the *work* of God and not have time for fellowship with Jesus. God help me not to be a slave to the thing in which I believe, but to have time to worship God!

The businessman has tensions, and demands on his time. Many times, because of his demands and tensions, the businessman may be a great influence in his community, but a slave to his business, having no time for God. I am not criticizing the purpose or work of the Lions Club, the Kiwanis Club, the Shriners, the Masons or any other such organization; but I know men who will climb a ten rail fence or go through a raging snowstorm to keep perfect attendance at their service clubs. These same men, some of them, will not bat an eye to get into the house of God. They are slaves to their perfect attendance when they should give God first place. He should come first and club work second.

Now, let's face it! There are some of you women who wouldn't miss that bridge club or that pink lemonade party for anything in the world. But you'll miss prayer meeting. You'll miss the missionary society meeting, except if they have a supper, and then you'll be there stirring the soup. But what we need is worship—putting things in their proper places so that God, our worship, and our relationship with Jesus come first. Jesus said that if we seek His Kingdom first all these other things will be added. Your business will still go on. You don't believe it? Remember this: You'll die some day, and things will just keep rolling on! So, bless God, they will roll better if you have fellowship with Jesus.

There are young people today who are going to college, and God knows that they are slaves. Marijuana, permissive sex, banner waving—they are out there parading, but they've never read their Bibles, they don't go to church. They have had a moral and spiritual breakdown.

They say they are there to get an education, yet one of the first things which was taught in my day was that young people in high school and college were to listen to all trends of thought and then make up their minds, not to sit and boo and yell, scream, parade and wave banners. I think the behavior of a lot of our students is a disgrace. Of course we have the right to express our opinions, but let's express them properly. Young people today are slaves, trying to get an education, but seriously in need of God in their program. Jesus would rebuke them if He were here today.

Martha possessed great ability to be a good hostess, but more than that—she didn't just possess this talent, it possessed her! There are men with money, and they don't own the money; the money owns them. Oh, the greed that is in their hearts for another dollar! They have a million, and they want two million; they have two million and they want ten million. There is greed in their hearts, and their boys and girls are slaves of "things."

Mary had no anxiety about dinner; she wasn't troubled. She knew that sooner or later they all were going to get something to eat. Mary had the secret—she was putting fellowship with Jesus first! She said, "Jesus is here. He is my guest. I love Him, and He is telling me something I want to hear from His lips." And He told her the things of God as they fellowshipped. She put first things first, and the other things took care of themselves. She wasn't anxious, she wasn't troubled. I am sure Mary helped many times in getting dinner. You know sisters; you know families. She was bound to have helped. But this time was different.

On a clear night, there are beautiful stars shining everywhere. Now, when the sun comes up in the morning the stars don't go away; they are still there, but we don't see them, because the light of the sun is so great that the stars take second place. When the Son of righteousness comes into the hearts of men and women, of boys and girls, everyday things don't just disappear; they are still there. You still have to go to work. You still have things which could trouble you, but they don't, because the Great One—Jesus—is there, and the greater minimizes the lesser. What we all need today is the confidence the Psalmist, David, had when he said, "The Lord is my shepherd." If you walk life's pathway with Him, you don't have to worry. Like the sheep, you know that He will take you to the green pastures when you get hungry. And when you get thirsty, He will take you to the still waters. And when you get bored, He will restore your soul.

That is what the Lord can do for you. Things will take their proper places because He will help you with them, and when you come to the end of the journey, you need not fear. "Yea, though I walk through the valley of the shadow of death, I will fear no evil: for thou art with me . . ." (Psalms 23:4). You will not have to cross Jordan alone. "And I will dwell in the house of the Lord forever" (Psalms 23:6).

Are you, like Martha, cumbered about many things? Then talk to Jesus about them. Come in like Mary did, to the feet of Jesus, and let Him minister and speak to you. Let Him bring you rest and help in every way.

10

Oak Tree Christians

*For by grace are ye saved through faith; and that
not of yourselves; it is the gift of God: Not of works,
lest any man should boast.* Ephesians 2:8, 9

As we learn to put first things first, we begin to grow as
Christians.

Not long ago a man came to me and said, "I'm not a bad
man. I go to church. I'm religious. I believe in God, and I believe
the Bible. I try to live right, but when I get around you fellows,
I realize that you have something I don't have."

He was a good man, but he said, "You have something I
don't have, and I'm interested in knowing more about it."

This is not a new story. It is quite an old one, in fact. When
Jesus was on earth, a man slipped through the quiet of the night
and came to Him—a man by the name of Nicodemus.

Nicodemus was a great religious man. He wore long robes,
fasted twice a week, and paid alms. He carefully followed the
laws and rituals of the church. But he came to Jesus and said,
"What is it You have, Lord? What's it all about?"

And Jesus answered, "Except a man be born again, he cannot
see the kingdom of God" (John 3:3).

What is involved when a person comes to Christ?

First, there is a negative side. The Bible says, "Old things
are passed away" (2 Corinthians 5:17).

The old things we once loved—pleasures, activities, even the crowd we used to run with—no longer attract us. We used to go out and get drunk, thinking we would have a good time, but we don't do that now.

We've come to the Lord, and we enjoy going to church, reading the Bible, praying and having fellowship with other Christians. Is that a good time? Try it! You'll find out that it is!

Some people, before they are born again, talk spitefully about their neighbors. They try to create strife, and every time you see them, they are like a wet blanket. Everything is derogatory. The things about which they talk are all negative.

But, when one comes to Jesus, if he is really born again, he has joy unspeakable. He is full of glory, and he spreads his joy wherever he goes. When people see him they say, "Here comes so-and-so, I'm glad to see him!" You can count on born-again people to spread a little sunshine, to tell others what the Lord has done for them. I hope you are that kind of Christian. If you are not, then God have mercy upon you!

The things which we once loved, we no longer care for when we have let Christ into our lives. The old sins, the old life—old things have passed away.

Then, there is a positive side: "Behold, I make all things new" (Revelation 21:5). It is the NEW life we have in Christ which makes the difference.

What this man who came to me was really saying was, "I've taken care of the negatives. I don't get drunk. I don't beat my wife. I don't rob any banks. I don't break the marriage vow. I operate my business on an honest, sound basis and don't cheat my fellowman. I'm a good man. I try to follow the rules and the ritual of the church. I believe in God!" Well, this is wonderful, as far as it goes, but if all he has today is a moral life, then he is lost.

God so loved the world that He gave His Son. There is only

one plan of salvation and that is God's plan—not your plan, not my plan, but God's plan. A part of this plan is negative—what we don't do; but the other part is positive—what we do.

This is where many people lose out. They recognize there is a God, that God loved us and gave His Son, but they have never accepted that love. They have never received the new life in Christ.

Man is a fallen race. He cannot be saved without a Saviour. We can pay all our debts, we can be kind to our wives and families, never gamble, never smoke, never lie, never steal, and still die and go to hell, because there is only one plan of salvation. That is God's plan: Jesus died that we might be redeemed and reconciled to God, and if we depend upon anything other than a Saviour, then we are lost people. That is according to the Scripture.

Christ is our only Saviour. All have sinned and come short of the glory of God; this includes each one of us. We are only sinners saved by grace. Were it not for the love of the Lord, every one of us would be lost. Salvation is a gift that we receive by faith. And when we come to Christ and we receive Him, old things do pass away—but all things also become new.

There are many people who would try to save themselves by not doing this or not doing that, but we can be saved only by the love of God, through Jesus Christ, with the Holy Spirit exalting Christ in our hearts and lives. When we receive Christ by faith, something happens. Not only do old things pass away, but new life develops. There are thousands of people who have never known that new life.

We must be *born again* before that new life can spring up. We'll never have the joy, the peace, or the things we really want and need spiritually until we have been born again, until we receive Christ and start living that new life.

In the Old Testament there is a story which clearly illustrates the difference between receiving Christ and just being good. A decision is what makes the difference.

Moses, one day, came to a crossroads in his life. He had the choice of doing either what the natural man would want to do—continue to be the son of Pharaoh's daughter and some day sit upon the throne, rule the army, and have great wealth in his hand—or doing what was right. The first thing he did was the negative; he refused to be called the son of Pharaoh's daughter.

The Egyptians kept the Israelites under bondage, forcing them to work as slaves in the mud pits. They lived vile lives, and worshipped false gods. Moses had the choice of going that way, but he said, "No, that is not for me. I am not going to go the way of the Egyptians."

Now, this was good, but it was not what God was really looking for in Moses' life (for God had called him).

He turned his back on the opportunity of one day becoming Egypt's ruler, choosing rather to suffer the affliction of the righteous for a season. But he not only took a negative step, by refusing the way of Egypt, he also took a positive one, by choosing the way of God.

You can be sure of this: When God closes His books, His dividends are greater than the devil ever thought about. His dividends are eternal.

There are many people today who need to refuse the sin, the habits, the doubts, the unbelief, and the old life they have, or else they will not be born again. First, they must receive Jesus Christ as their Saviour. Then, they must strengthen the activities in their lives that bear witness to the fact that they are believers in Him—by acting like, talking like, and associating with the people who are on their way to Heaven, not those on their way to hell.

God had given Moses a duty to perform, which was to lead

the children of Israel out of the mud pits of Egypt. Because Moses made the right decision, he became the world's greatest deliverer of mankind.

There are thousands of people today who say, "Oh, I believe in God, I believe in Jesus," but that is as far as they go. They are like Nicodemus—they have for themselves righteousness, but they are searching for life eternal, joy unspeakable, and the peace of God in their souls.

There is a positive act they must perform, which is to receive God's plan of salvation as the beginning. Then, there is a follow-up: Salvation is more than giving up; salvation is also *receiving what God has promised us.*

Now, how did Moses distinguish right from wrong? He knew he had to make a choice. It would have been easy for him to say to himself, "Well, now, for the present at least, Egypt offers me fame and fortune, and that's what I want."

But Moses saw the eternal side, and balanced his books in the light of eternity. He knew that Egypt could offer only temporary blessings, where God Almighty offered eternal life.

Sin may look like an angel right now, but sin is a devil for eternity—don't forget it! Too many people like the bright lights and the "good times" sin offers, but the end of it is the way of death. When Moses began to weigh these things, he concluded that ". . . the reproach of Christ [is] greater riches than the treasures in Egypt: for he had respect unto the recompense of the reward" (Hebrews 11:26).

What was the outcome of Moses' decision? He encountered suffering, heartache, and disappointment—but finally, he led the children of Israel out of Egypt.

Now, first of all, he himself was blessed. He saw God in the burning bush, and God spoke to him. Oh, it is wonderful to have God minister to us individually!

Second, Moses knew the will of God, and led the Israelites out of the mud pits of Egypt. He not only made a personal dedication, but he became a blessing to the human race.

God wants to make all of us a blessing to someone else—winning someone to the Lord, praying for someone in need, carrying someone else's burden. Christian service is essential in a Christian life.

Moses' decision also gave him a home in Heaven and set him apart. We read in the Book of Hebrews that Moses was listed among the most faithful. "By faith Moses . . . refused to be called the son of Pharaoh's daughter; Choosing rather to suffer affliction with the people of God, than to enjoy the pleasures of sin for a season; . . . By faith he forsook Egypt. . . . Through faith he kept the passover. . . . By faith they passed through the Red Sea as by dry land" (Hebrews 11:24–29).

And because Moses chose to serve the Lord, he was named as one of the faithful in God's great Book.

Moses made his decision and found an eternal home. One day when Jesus was here on earth, He took those in His inner circle—Peter, James and John—to the Mount of Transfiguration. There appeared on that Mount with Jesus, Elijah, and who else? Who else was there? Moses!

If you could ask, "Moses, did you make the right decision years ago?," he would reply, "Where is the money and wealth of Egypt? Where are the Pharaohs today? They are dead and all buried. Where is the army? It has drowned in the sea. But look at me. I have a glorified body. I'm having fellowship with Jesus. I'm going to live eternally in the Kingdom of God."

Let us remember: If we make the right decisions, they will pay in eternity, not just in life. Some people have had a difficult time serving the Lord down here. Their relatives and the ungodly people they work with on their jobs have given them a hard time. But it will be worth it all when they see Jesus.

One day, a little acorn fell off a big oak tree onto the ground. Rain fell. The sun shone. After a while a little sprout formed. It looked up at the tree from which it had fallen and said, "I'm an oak tree, I'm an oak tree!"

The big oak tree looked down and said, "No, you're not an oak tree yet."

The next year the sprout grew a little more, and it said, "I'm an oak tree, I'm an oak tree!" but again the big oak said, "Not yet; you're not an oak tree yet."

The little sprout grew and grew, until its branches were entwined with those of the big tree.

Then one day there came a terrible storm. Hail fell, lightning flashed, winds blew. The big oak and the little oak swayed back and forth. Limbs were broken off, leaves fell.

Finally, when the storm had subsided, the little oak again looked at the big oak—and this time the big oak said, "Now, you are an oak tree."

Our victory is not assured until we have fought the battles of life and stood the storms of time, entwined with Jesus Christ.

Then, some day, when we stand in His presence, we shall have victory! We shall be oak trees! And throughout eternity, we shall be Christ-followers, Christlike, truly Christian!

How often you and I look up and say, "Lord, I'm a Christian." Then the storms of life come and show us the true depth we have in Him.

My friend, do not put stock in what you do or don't do. Put your trust in Christ, in what He did on Calvary and what He can do in your life right now.

The arm of flesh will fail you, but the arm of the Lord is mighty to save. If you are going through a severe storm and your life is being tested, remember the little oak tree: Hold onto the Lord and be faithful, for He will give you a crown of life.

11

Will You Be There?

I delight to do thy will, O my God: yea, thy law is within my heart. I have preached righteousness in the great congregation: lo, I have not refrained my lips, O Lord, thou knowest. I have not hid thy righteousness within my heart; I have declared thy faithfulness and thy salvation: I have not concealed thy lovingkindness and thy truth from the great congregation.

Psalms 40:8–10

"And the word of the Lord came unto him, [Elijah] saying, Get thee hence, and turn thee eastward, and hide thyself by the brook Cherith, that is before Jordan. And it shall be, that thou shalt drink of the brook; and I have commanded the ravens to feed thee there . . . And the word of the Lord came unto him, saying, Arise, get thee to Zarephath, which belongeth to Zidon, and dwell there: behold, I have commanded a widow woman there to sustain thee" (1 Kings 17:2–4, 8–9).

Ahab was the king, but, influenced by his wife Jezebel, he had become very wicked. One day, Elijah, the prophet, walked up to Ahab and declared, "I'm going to get down on my knees, look to my God, and ask Him to shut up the heavens and not let it rain." Now, this is pretty bold language, even for a man of God. But the situation required bold language, because Ahab and Jezebel had led the people away from God. And I tell you, it is about time, today, that the people who love God, who believe in God and serve Him, stand up and be counted for Him! Too much is being said in newspapers, on radio and TV against belief in God. God's people need to stand up and declare that there *is* a God, who is on His throne, who is very much alive!

"And Elijah the Tishbite, who was of the inhabitants of Gilead, said unto Ahab, as the Lord God of Israel liveth, before whom I stand, there shall not be dew nor rain these years, but according to my word" (1 Kings 17:1). Then he walked off, and as soon as he had gone, Ahab and all his men began saying that Elijah was a fanatic, mentally unbalanced. But God told Elijah to go and hide by the brook Cherith, and that the ravens would feed him there.

My friend, there is not a place on the face of the earth that God would have fed Elijah by a raven other than the brook Cherith. He said, "I will feed you *there*." Elijah could not change God's plan or God's purpose, any more than you or I can change them.

Don't get me wrong. When we sin and do wrong, we change God's plan for our lives, because of our sin. But God had made Elijah a promise, and God's promises are in accordance with His plan for our lives.

We cannot change God's plan. God says, "I'll meet you *there*." He didn't tell Elijah that He would meet him just anywhere— "I'll meet you *there*."

Now, after a while the brook dried up, because there had been no rain. And God told Elijah to go to Zarephath, where a widow woman would give him food. God provided for Elijah at the brook Cherith, because He promised to; He provided for him at the widow woman's house, because He promised to. But Elijah had to do what God told him, or God's promises did not have to be fulfilled. In fact, God's promises *would not* have been fulfilled had Elijah gone to some other place.

In the Old Testament, we read of Jacob and how he went down to Bethel, how he wandered off, and then, finally, was in trouble. God told Jacob to go back to Bethel and rebuild the altar and that He would meet him there. Jacob went to Bethel and rebuilt the altar and God did meet him there, because He had promised. Likewise, today God can give a witness in our hearts and meet us in our hour of need.

The shepherd boy David—God met him at his "there." As the giant stood uttering blasphemous curses, making fun of the children of God, this boy said, "Who does he think he is? Somebody must go get him." David's *"there"* was in his heart. He had a promise that he could take care of that giant, and he did, with a little slingshot.

The Cathedral of Tomorrow's "there" was the day God laid the burden on our heart to stay in one community and build a church. This was our "there." We could have continued what we were doing and have won some souls, but I believe the ministry God has given us here would not be in existence if we had not met our "there." And God has proved Himself true! We rejoice in our church, in our television ministry; but more than that, His Spirit. His power and presence have been with us—God has given us thousands of souls at our altars. To God be the glory! It is not the work of man; it is the work of the Lord! God made the promise, and we met Him as He asked. Believe me, He is still keeping His promises!

He promised to open doors throughout America, into every state in the Union. I preached this twenty years ago, when we incorporated and had only two stations. Today our televised service reaches into every state and from coast to coast across Canada. I believe it was God's plan, not Rex Humbard's. I believe we must be true to our calling and be where God places us, if we want God's promises. And God has also raised up many listeners and readers as our partners in faith, in prayer, in giving, in believing.

On the other hand, I believe there are many people in our own community and throughout our audiences who are not where they belong with God in soul-winning. I believe God has called people all across this nation to bind themselves together in faith and prayer, to believe for a revival in our generation. I believe if just the Christians reading this book would get on their faces before God—would fast and pray—that God would throw off the shackles of sin and give America such a revival that we would hear the Lord being glorified on every hill and in every valley in America.

We CAN have revival in our generation! I am convinced that He called us, that He placed us here, that He gave us a church, that He gave us an open door to television, and gave us a promise of great revival. I am expecting, I am believing for a great revival! Somehow, I can hear the rumbling in the mulberry trees (2 Samuel 5:24). I can hear the abundance of rain (1 Kings 18:41). I've seen the cloud the size of a man's hand (1 Kings 18:44) . . . I believe that God is still on the throne, and God has not lost His power. He can and does answer prayer!

I say to you, in America, in Canada, the world over: Our churches need a revival. Christians need a revival. Our ministers need an old-fashioned, Holy Ghost, God-sent, soul-saving revival—until our hearts burn to see souls saved, until our eyes shed tears for the lost, for the sick, for the suffering, and for the dying. The whole world wants and needs this.

We find that Elijah, the man of God, spent three years in his "there," and God provided for him at Cherith and at the widow's house. But then came that day when God's word came, telling him to go back to see Ahab. He went, and Obadiah came running down the road. Now, Obadiah had great faith in God, but he had aligned himself with the wrong crowd. He was out looking for grass when we should have been on his knees praying for rain. I tell you, the Church of the Lord Jesus Christ has been doing the same thing—looking for grass when we should have been praying for revival. This is the day and the hour when we have everything but real revival. When I say revival I'm not talking about protracted meetings; I'm talking about something real. I'm talking about a service where God is glorified and sinners are saved; where Christians get on fire and get rid of their sinful habits; where they are sanctified, Spirit-filled, and thenceforth live for the Lord.

Today we worry about how to fill our churches. Too often our churches, instead of having revival and winning souls to the Kingdom, have been just a bunch of people out looking for grass. The world is going to hell. It doesn't care a thing about what we are doing; and we are out looking for grass instead of praying for the rain that will produce the grass—and by that I mean a revival. God get us back to looking for the rain and the showers from heaven! God give us a revival in America! I believe we can have it!

Elijah went to Ahab, and "Ahab said unto him, Art thou he that troubleth Israel? And he answered, I have not troubled Israel; but thou, and thy father's house, in that ye have forsaken the commandments of the Lord . . ." (1 Kings 18:17–18). Isn't that just like people—"Art thou he that troubleth Israel?" I can hear someone right now saying, "That old Calamity Jane, Rex Humbard; why doesn't he calm down?" The devil would like to lull us to sleep. But, my friend, we had better get excited while we have the opportunity. Time is running out!

Elijah said it was sin which was troubling Israel, and he challenged Ahab to bring his prophets and come to Mount Carmel. "Build your altar," he taunted. "Pray to your God and see what happens."

You know the rest of the story—how the worshippers of Baal prayed in vain for their god to send down fire, and how, when Elijah prayed, "the fire of the Lord fell, and consumed the burnt sacrifice, and the wood, and the stones, and the dust, and licked up the water that was in the trench" (1 Kings 18:38).

We aren't going to solve the problems in our streets, we aren't going to solve the problems of juvenile delinquency, we aren't going to solve *any* problems by laws and their enforcement. Our problems will be solved only when we get right with God! If ministers would get in their pulpits and preach against sin, if people would clean up their lives, we would minimize our problems in America. That doesn't set too well, but it is the truth.

Elijah built an altar unto God. Let us rebuild our altars in our homes; let us build and use the altars of our churches. Let us learn what a prayer room really is, and what intercessory prayer can do. When Zion travails, she shall bring forth sons and daughters. God's promise is true! So, Elijah prayed and the fire fell, and when the supernatural happened, all the people said, "The Lord, he is the God" (1 Kings 18:39)!

Elijah was there, where God wanted him to be, at the time God wanted him to be there, and God kept His promise! I believe we are right here, where God wants us to be. Let us stay, and build, and believe together! Let us pray for revival in this our generation. I believe we are here because God said, "Go there!" We have done what we have because that is what God said to do. Now, let us expect the sound of the abundance of rain, and anticipate the supernatural!

12

God Is Not Dead
. . . the Church Is Dead
and Buried in Ritual

Wilt thou not revive us again: that thy people may rejoice in thee? Shew us thy mercy, O Lord, and grant us thy salvation. I will hear what God the Lord will speak: for he will speak peace unto his people, and to his saints: but let them not turn again to folly. Surely his salvation is nigh them that fear him; that glory may dwell in our land. Psalms 85:6-9

Once I knew a young lady who was very beautiful. She was in the prime of life. She was married, and she and her husband were very happy. She was the type of person whom you could look at and know that she was a little above the average; she stood out from among the crowd.

After a while this young couple moved to a community which was too far away to drive regularly to the Cathedral services. I did not see them for quite a few years. Then one day a phone message came, calling me to the hospital. When I entered the room, I saw two beds. I looked for the person as I remembered her, but I didn't recognize anyone in that room. Then I called the name, and one of them said, "That's me." Her cheeks were hollow; her arms were nothing but skin over bones. I went over to talk with her. The story was that the terrible, dreaded disease called cancer had taken away her beauty and replaced it with hollow spots; had taken the sparkle out of her eyes and replaced it with pain and suffering. That smile, that complexion, that look which she once had—all were gone. Just skin and bones remained.

As I stand in the pulpit each Sunday, I recall the beauty of the early New Testament Church; the power of God that was present, where the anointing of the Spirit was so great that three thousand souls were added to the Lord in one day, and five thousand another day, where the sick leaped for joy, where Peter and John took by the hand the lame man from the gate called Beautiful and said, "Silver and gold have I none; but such as I have give I thee: In the name of Jesus Christ of Nazareth rise up and walk" (Acts 3:6).

I see the joy of the Lord in these disciples as persecution set in. They refused to be silenced by the authorities: "And now, Lord, behold their threatenings: and grant unto thy servants, that with all boldness they may speak thy word . . . And when they had prayed, the place was shaken where they were assembled together; and they were all filled with the Holy Ghost, and they spake the word of God with boldness" (Acts 4:29, 31). And they went in every direction. What a great revival! In the New Testament, I see the power of God.

But as I look upon the Church of the Lord Jesus Christ today, it reminds me of that woman in the hospital. The exuberance seems to be gone; the power and the anointing to deliver people of their sins and bad habits seem to be gone; the joy has been lost out of the Church. We need an old-fashioned, Holy Ghost, God-fearing, soul-saving, spirit-filled revival today, that we might be restored unto the faith that was once delivered unto the saints.

Today, no announcement could shock an average congregation or create less enthusiasm, less approval, and less expectancy than to have the minister stand up and say, "This week we will begin a revival campaign." The effect is like a sudden chilling wind! Everyone rejoices in other kinds of revival. We find joy in physical revival—getting healed and getting well, but not in a spiritual revival!

We rejoice in a revival of business. We always like to get a little higher wages and a better price for our goods. We always want conditions a little better. If business has a little slump, we agitate for a revival. Then why shouldn't we want a revival in God, in religion, and in faith?

You say, "Well, now, Rex, you are a little old-fashioned. You believe in old-fashioned things, and we are living in a modern world." Well, I think you are a little old-fashioned, too. Adam and Eve were breathing in the Garden of Eden, and you are still breathing. Why don't you quit it? Adam and Eve were eating in the Garden of Eden, and you are still eating. Why don't you quit it? It is not old-fashioned to believe for revival today. We need God to do something for our souls, just as much as our bodies need air to breathe and food to eat. We need a revival!

If we ever needed a revival of faith in God and of religion, it is now! We want revival in science, we want it in medicine, we want it in physical things, in business and in nature. But when we say something about "let's have a revival in spiritual things," the reply is, "Not me, I'm too busy, I don't have time, I don't need anything." Everyone is too complacent!

The modern church is an easy-going church. Its members are comfortable, content, and not willing to pay the price. They don't particularly care to be dead, but they would rather be dead than to do anything about it. They have lost the joy of the Lord. They have lost all spirituality. They love the things of the world. They have no love for their fellowman, their brother. Yet, they are satisfied to come to church, to go through the ritual, and to receive absolutely nothing that will improve their sickened condition.

We have lost power, we have lost strength, and the Church of Jesus Christ in general today is as bad as that woman in the hospital. At one time she had beauty, but she became sick and weak. She endured suffering, and she never revived. Not many days after I saw her, we stood beside her grave and laid her to rest.

I wonder how many reading this chapter will be laid to rest spiritually, travel on in sin, let their boys and girls go to hell, let their neighbors and friends never come to a saving knowledge of Jesus Christ. Hosea, in the Old Testament, said, ". . . break up your fallow ground: for it is time to seek the Lord, till he come and rain righteousness upon you" (Hosea 10:12). Hosea must have been a farmer, because a farmer goes out and breaks up the soil and the ground, that he might do something. What? Plant the seed!

It is time for you and me to get down on our knees and weep before the Lord and hold on to the horns of the altar. It is time for us to break up the fallow ground of our hearts, that the Word of God might be planted, that we might study the Word and have the anointing of the Lord upon the Word, that it might grow and blossom and bear fruit in the form of spiritual revival.

Hosea knew what the trouble was: Vows had been broken. And people today say, "God, I'll live for you; I'll pay my tithes; I'll pray; I'll read my Bible." But we get so busy that we forget our vows. We need to return to the Lord!

The Bible says, ". . . for as soon as Zion travailed, she brought forth her children" (Isaiah 66:8). It doesn't say maybe somebody would happen to be saved, maybe someone would be born to the Kingdom by chance, but *when the Church travails!* I wonder how long it has been since Christians who are reading this have got down on their knees and held on to God for the souls of their boys, their girls, their neighbors, their friends and the ones with whom they work? How many have prayed until they cried and wept in travail, in agonizing prayer! How long has it been since you have prayed like *you* should be praying daily?

God give us a church that will be indued with power from on high, that will have a burden for the lost, that will win the lost at any cost—it matters not how much time it may take in prayer and in faith. Today, we need some people who will say, "Wilt thou not revive us again: that thy people may rejoice in thee" (Psalms 85:6)? You don't see very many victorious Christians, and it is because they need a revival in their own souls. When we have a revival, we have victorious Christians.

One day a man went to a baseball game. He sat there and holloed. He had a good time; he enjoyed the game. Suddenly, he felt a little bit strange and began to get dizzy. When he tried to get up his legs wouldn't work. Then he found his arms wouldn't work. So they took him home and learned that he had had a stroke. They could stick a pin in him and he couldn't even feel it. Now, they didn't call in all of his friends and start rejoicing that he had had a stroke. What do you think they did? Why, they called a doctor.

If there ever was a time when the Church in general has been paralyzed in doing the will of God, it is now. And the Church can't rejoice when it is paralyzed. We should call on the Great Physician, who is able to help us. We need a revival that will restore and give back the strength, the power and the anointing.

I want to tell you something! GOD *IS NOT* DEAD; He is still on the throne; He still hears and answers prayer! The God of Elijah is still alive, and He is looking for some Elijahs! The God of Peter and Paul is still alive, and He is looking for some Peters and Pauls! The God of Abraham and Isaac and Jacob is still alive. The God of your grandmother and grandfather is still alive. The

God who answers prayer is still on the throne; He is just looking for someone to pray, someone to believe, someone to trust! May God help us to be those people who believe, who pray, and who trust! The Church *should not rejoice* in the face of its calamity and its paralyzed condition; it should *get on its face* and call out to God and pray until He restores and gives revival. *That* will be the time to rejoice!

Ezekiel spoke to a bunch of dead bones, and God Almighty brought them together, put skin on them and gave them flesh and breathed into them life. I hate to say this because I am a pastor, but I want to tell you something: As I look at the Church in the world today I'm looking at a bunch of skeletons that need skin and flesh, that need life breathed into them by God Almighty. It was not Ezekiel who did it—it was God! And it will not be man who will bring revival; it will be God who does it— when man obeys God.

Ezekiel said that God prophesied. I believe the Lord called me to preach and to say, "We're going to have a revival; we're going to believe for revival; we're going to believe for spiritual power, for spiritual anointing, and for great rejoicing and great joy!" And I believe we can have it!

Restore—give back. Joel's prophecy said, "I will restore." The Church needs to have restored unto it power and joy, anointing, and a burden and compassion. But first of all we must repent! Then we'll have revival!

13

"There Is Death in the Pot"
... There Is Poison in the Church

And Elisha came again to Gilgal: and there was a dearth in the land; and the sons of the prophets were sitting before him: and he said unto his servant, Set on the great pot, and seethe pottage for the sons of the prophets. And one went out into the field to gather herbs, and found a wild vine, and gathered thereof wild gourds his lap full, and came and shred them into the pot of pottage: for they knew them not. So they poured out for the men to eat: and it came to pass, as they were eating of the pottage, that they cried out, and said, O thou man of God, there is death in the pot. And they could not eat thereof. But he said, Then bring meal. And he cast it into the pot; and he said, Pour out for the people that they may eat. And there was no harm in the pot. 2 Kings 4:38–41

Here is a simple story, but a wonderful one for drawing a parallel with the day in which we live.

The sons of the prophet had what we would call today a convention, or a state or national meeting of their church. When it came time to eat, they were served some pottage. Suddenly someone said, "There is poison here! There is something in here that doesn't belong, and it is detrimental to our lives."

104

When he heard this, the servant of the Lord asked for some meal. He stirred it into the pottage and the poison was removed— by the supernatural power of God Almighty!

Now as we think about this for a moment we realize this was a place for Elisha and the others to get their physical nourishment. And today, the Church is where people come together for their spiritual nourishment. Since Christ came and died, ascended into the heavens and sent His Spirit upon all flesh, the Gospel has become something for everyone to come and partake of—whether he be Jew or Gentile, it makes no difference. All are to come and receive from the Lord that sufficient part they need.

Now, just as someone in Elisha's day threw poison in to destroy the wholesome food, we in the hour in which we live have had poison thrown into our spiritual food—into the Gospel of Jesus Christ.

It is easy for us to want to blame somebody for poison besides ourselves. It would have been easy for someone to say, "This is the guy who threw those poisonous gourds into the food." But all who had anything to do with this were responsible. Not only the man who put the poison in, but also the men who failed to examine what was being put in. They failed to detect the things that would be destructive and would not build up and give health and strength. Then, the man who ate suffered all day. He might not be directly responsible, but he was involved because of what happened at his place of nourishment.

To illustrate, one guy makes the liquor, another sells it, and still another drinks it. Then, under the influence of it, the one who drank it has a wreck on the highway and kills someone, or he beats his wife and kids. Well, a certain amount of responsibility goes to the fellows who made and sold it; and a certain amount goes to the fellow who drank it. Or, you go sit down in some public place—a restaurant, a train, or airplane—and some-

one blows smoke in your face from a cancer weed. The guy who
made it is responsible; the guy who sold it is responsible; and
the guy who is smoking it is responsible—not only for his own
health, but also for the health of those around him. He is intrud-
ing on their privacy.

Now I don't want anyone to get the idea I am after the modernists, and leaving the fundamentalists alone. You could not
have the modernist progress if the people in the Church would
preach the Truth, and live it.

There has come a great falling away in the world in which
we live. A falling away from what? From believing in the supernatural power of God! We haven't fallen away from building
programs; we haven't fallen away from social activities; but we
have fallen away from the Truth that we must have a "born-
again" experience or we are not in the Kingdom of God.

I believe there are some good people and some bad people in
all the denominations. There are some Spirit-filled people in the
Cathedral of Tomorrow, and there are others who need God,
and who hunger for more of God.

We don't just want to look out yonder and point a finger at
some that we might say are the liberals and the modernists and
condemn them. Let's turn back to the ones who are responsible,
because we have not practiced what we have preached.

Every person who claims to be a Christian, and who has habits
in his or her life which displease God has a poison that can kill
the Gospel we preach. Every person who has dedicated his or her
life to God and yet is not telling others what Christ means is a
detriment and a poison to the Gospel of Jesus Christ. Every
Christian who is not a tither, giving one dollar out of every ten
to God's work and the winning of souls, is a detriment to pro-
viding the right distribution of the Bread of Life.

I am not jumping on any denomination. If the leadership of
a church believes in the Gospel, preaches it and practices it, you

can expect the members of that church to do the same, regardless of what the denomination is. But you cannot have a man who denies Bible teaching stand in a pulpit, and expect to have a spiritual church.

You can't substitute anything else for a born-again experience. You can't substitute any "social gospel" or any "sociable gospel" for your faith that God's Word *is* God's Word. We do need social concern and sociability, but we must not neglect the real heart.

You have a mind, a body and a soul. You can straighten out the mind and the body, but if you don't get that soul right with God you are a lost sinner. Believe the fundamental truths of the Bible: There is a God. The Bible is God's inspired Word. Jesus Christ is the only Saviour.

Why do we have the increase in crime? Why are the divorce courts filled? Why are many churches nearly empty? Because we do not have the leadership we need! Theological seminaries turn out men who deny Bible Truth. Here again is a responsibility that must be shared; this condition is the responsibility not only of the theological seminaries, and the ministers who deny the Truth, but also of the people who believe the Truth and haven't had enough sense to rally around and project this Truth into the world in which we live, until it will crowd out the unbelief.

We who belong to the National Association of Evangelicals—if we have not been out pioneering, preaching, and lifting up the blood-stained banner of Jesus Christ, then we are as guilty as the man who denies the Truth.

To support programs that do not advocate the fundamental Truth is to be guilty of supporting something else. To do nothing is to lend support to denial of the Truth.

I am not fighting the denominations here, but rather I would be a friend like the doctor in this illustration:

Suppose I have blood poisoning in my little finger. I know that if I don't do something it will spread into my hand, and from there up into my arm and into my whole body, and finally kill me. So I go to the doctor.

Now, would that doctor be my friend if he said, "I like you, Rex, and I don't want to do anything to hurt you; so—I'm just going to leave it alone"?

No, of course that doctor would not be my friend. The friend would be the doctor who would say, "Rex, we've tried everything we can, and the poison is still there and spreading. I want you to get ready for an operation; I'm going to cut off that blood poison from your body."

Recently, I went into a hospital to see a man who had lost one of his legs. The doctors had amputated it to try to save his life. Now, no one wants to have a leg cut off. But if a person is going to die if it isn't done, then I think the doctor is a friend to remove that leg that the person might live.

In its issue of October 13, 1967, *Christianity Today* reported on a survey made by an independent organization. I am going to tell you some things they found out about what present-day ministers believe. As a friend, I am using these statistics because I am called by God Almighty to warn you, "Rid yourself of that blood poison, or you are going to die." As long as I am alive, there will be at least one loud-mouthed preacher crying out against the apostasy of this day.

In the survey, a Western Reserve University sociologist, Jeffery Haden, contacted 10,000 Protestant clergymen in the United States. Out of the 10,000, 7,441 replied.

The first question the ministers were asked was: "Do you believe in Jesus' physical resurrection from the grave, in the same sense that you believe Abraham Lincoln was assassinated?" In other words, do you believe Jesus' resurrection from the grave is a historical fact?

Here is the answer: "Fifty-one percent of the Methodist

ministers in the United States said they did not accept the resurrection from the grave as historical fact; 30 percent of the Episcopal priests did not accept it; 35 percent of the United Presbyterian preachers did not accept it; 33 percent of the American Baptist preachers; 13 percent of the American Lutheran preachers; and 7 percent of the Missouri Synod of Lutheran ministers did not accept this."

Do you know what they are saying? They are saying they do not believe the prophecies of the Old Testament which said that He would come, would suffer, would die, then would be resurrected. This is the very heart of the Gospel.

Now read this, from the same survey:

When asked if they believed in the virgin birth of Jesus Christ as a biological miracle, 60 percent of the American Methodist preachers said no; 44 percent of the Episcopal priests did not believe in it. Neither did 49 percent of the Lutheran ministers in the Missouri Synod, along with 19 percent of the American Lutheran ministers.

But the most alarming finding of this poll is this:

When asked if they believed in the Bible as God's inspired Word, 82 percent of the Methodist preachers rejected the inspiration of the Bible. So did 89 percent of the Episcopal priests, 81 percent of the Presbyterian clergy, 57 percent of the American Baptist clergy, and 57 percent of the American Lutheran clergy.

Now, we are trying to feed people the common faith that was once delivered unto the saints. Along comes this great percentage of people, and, because of unbelief, poison is thrown into the pot. Then we try to feed the spiritually hungry from the poisoned Gospel.

I advocate that every person reading this book uphold the principles of the Bible as God's inspired Word. Fellowship with the people who teach it, and practice it.

I am not an enemy of the Gospel of Jesus Christ, and I am

not an enemy of the Church of Jesus Christ. I am a friend who says, "Let us remove the poison from the Gospel we are preaching to the world."

When the prophet of the Lord found that there was poison in the pot, he asked for meal, and threw it in, and the supernatural power of the Almighty God removed the poison.

The only thing that will remove the poison in the hearts and minds of the modernists who call themselves Christians—whether in the pulpit or in the pew—is to throw in the Bread of Life, the Reality, the Truth, and to have it in our lives, so it can be an example to offset those who do not believe.

I call upon each one of you to identify yourself with the people who believe the fundamental Truth of the Word of God. Support this kind of program for God; lift up the hands of those who are preaching the Truth.

If we do this, we can get a job done that will offset the negative and the bad which we have in the world today. We need to return to that faith that was once delivered to the saints: God is alive! The Gospel works, and it is stimulating!

If you have sinful habits, and you call yourself a Christian or identify with the people of God, those habits are detrimental, and are poison to the Gospel. Those of you who have doubts and fears, your anxieties and lack of trust are poison to the Gospel. Those of you who are not sure of your home in Heaven, if even though you have gone to church for many years you are not sure that you have been born again—it is time to have an experience with God. Know whom you belong to, and where you are going. Until you do, until you shed your sins and the things that are wrong, you will continue to be detrimental.

O God, we do not hide the things that are wrong in the church. Do examine the hearts and lives of men and women, boys and girls. Don't let us be guilty of not believing the supernaturally

inspired *Word of God—of not believing in the need of a born-
again experience for each follower of the risen Christ. Lord, add
to our numbers, and may thy children be as you would have them
be—upholding the faith so that the hungry world might find
nourishment rather than poison. In the name of our Saviour we
pray. Amen.*

14

Where Are the Miracles Today?

And the angel of the Lord appeared unto him, and said unto him, The Lord is with thee, thou mighty man of valour. And Gideon said unto him, Oh my Lord, if the Lord be with us, why then is all this befallen us? and where be all his miracles which our fathers told us of, saying, Did not the Lord bring us up from Egypt? but now the Lord hath forsaken us, and delivered us into the hands of the Midianites. And the Lord looked upon him, and said, Go in this thy might, and thou shalt save Israel from the hand of the Midianites: have not I sent thee? And he said unto him, Oh my Lord, wherewith shall I save Israel? behold, my family is poor in Manasseh, and I am the least in my father's house. And the Lord said unto him, Surely I will be with thee, and thou shalt smite the Midianites as one man. Judges 6:12–16

The Lord works in wondrous and mysterious ways. In this passage, God is not talking to a great chief of state, but to a humble farmer.

It was a dark time for the Jewish nation. They had sinned against God, and now were under the heel of the Midianite army.

The enemy was everywhere, robbing the Israelites of their

cattle and crops; but that didn't stop Gideon. He pitched a few bundles of wheat down into an old wine press, and there he threshed out what little grain he could while hiding from the Midianite soldiers.

I can see the old boy down there, beating the stalks with his hands and feet, trying to get the grain separated from the straw. He was raising quite a lot of dust with all that pounding, but his doubts and fears were rising higher than the dust. Every once in a while, he would look out over the rim of the wine press to see if the enemy had spotted him.

Suddenly, the angel of the Lord appeared unto him and said, "The Lord is with thee, thou mighty man of valor."

The angel's voice stopped Gideon cold. "Me? A man of valor?"

"Wait a minute," he said. "Wait just a minute. The facts don't bear out what you are saying, Mr. Angel. If the Lord be with me, and with Israel, then where are the miracles of the days gone by?

"What about the time He rolled the Red Sea back for Moses and the children of Israel? When they were hungry, He fed them manna from Heaven. And when they were thirsty, He had Moses bring water out of the rock.

"We never see miracles like that today. We're defeated and our enemy is strong. They take anything that strikes their fancy. If God is for us, why have all these things befallen us?"

Gideon didn't seem to have too much faith in what the angel of the Lord had to say. He was full of questions, and blamed God for the condition of his nation, Israel.

Nevertheless, the name of this doubting farmer would go down in the annals of faith, in the Word of God, along with such great men as Daniel, David, and the three men in the fiery furnace: Shadrach, Meshach, and Abednego. Just as their faith won victories, Gideon's faith would see him through to victory over the Midianites.

If a man like Gideon—afraid and blaming God for his troubles —could be changed, you and I can be changed, too.

If there ever was a time we needed change, it is now! Everywhere we turn there is violence, from riots to full-scale war. Our streets aren't safe to walk on because of the high incidence of crime. One out of every three marriages is ending in the divorce courts. Drug addiction is exploding into epidemic proportions.

We are continually hearing today from the skeptics, the unbelievers, the doubters: "If there is a God who cares, then why have all these things happened?"

This is basically the same question Gideon asked. The answer does not really depend upon God's action, for He is already willing to come on the scene of human need and work miracles. The responsibility lies in the hearts of the people of God. Like Israel, you and I today have made it impossible for God to work because of our sin.

We have built altars unto ourselves. We have done things in our own way. We have broken His laws. Then, we look up and blame God for all the trouble, for the mess the world is in!

It is not God who is on trial, but you and I. The trouble is not God's fault. He has laid down the pattern for us to follow, but we have sinned and gone our own way.

Man lives his life as though God does not exist. His faith goes no further than his own abilities. As a result, we stand seemingly paralyzed in the face of today's mounting problems.

In Gideon's day, there were those who stood around and said, "There's no need of planting, gathering, or threshing the wheat. What's the use? The enemy will only come and take it."

But Gideon stayed busy. In spite of his doubts and fears, he kept threshing his wheat; and God saw fit to use him. If you want to see God move in your midst, you must first believe there is a God. You must not only believe God is, but that He is all powerful, that there is no power He cannot conquer, that all things are possible with Him.

You must have a life-changing experience with God, and then move out by faith and begin to grow in the Lord. And when this happens, you will begin to see the miracles.

Often people will say to me, "I'd live for God if it were not for my wife, or my husband, or the fact there are so many hypocrites in the church." They say, "I try to live for God, but Satan comes in and stops me."

How can God work in your life when you go around and brag about the power of the devil like that? God is far more powerful than anything the devil can put in our way.

These folks are just making excuses why they can't serve God. They build little altars to their idols of "because," and "if." When they get caught in a sin, they cry, "The devil made me do it." That little slogan is really bragging on the devil.

People wait for God to bless them. They refuse to put their faith into action. But faith demands action. My Bible tells me that faith without works is dead. It also says that without faith it is impossible to please God.

A young man came into my office recently and said, "You know, I feel the Lord wants me to go out in evangelistic work." He explained what great things he could do for the Lord as an evangelist. I looked him straight in the eye and said, "I've known you for many years. The thing you really need is to get down to the business at hand—witnessing and winning souls for Jesus right where you are. It can be in Sunday school or in personal evangelism. You need to stop bouncing around and get busy for God."

"Oh, I want a big job to do," he said. "I don't want a little job."

I have news for you, my friend: There are no big shots in

God's work. If you aren't willing to do the least of the little jobs, then you'll never do the big ones.

When Gideon believed and put his faith in God, he was willing to do whatever the Lord had for him. Then God made him part of the solution rather than part of the problem.

The Midianites lived by a grove of trees on a hill so thickly wooded that people on the outside couldn't see the adultery and other evil deeds that were going on in the grove.

These people wanted a God who would live among their sins. They were not interested in the true and holy God so they built an altar unto Baal.

When Gideon realized that something had to be done and that God was with him, the first thing he did was to jump up in the middle of the night and grab his ax. He took along 10 men and went up that hill, and all night long they were cutting down trees in the grove so there was no place for the people to hide their sin. The next thing he did was to go over and tear down the altars of Baal. Then, right out there in the middle of hell, so to speak, he built an altar unto the true and the living God.

The next morning when the people got up, they had no grove and no altar—Baal had died! And they found an altar built unto God.

I tell you, I feel like getting an ax and doing some chopping myself. I feel like building an altar, for God is alive and on His throne! He hears and answers prayer! If we would believe and fight like Gideon, we would see that God is not dead, but very much alive!

The Bible says the Spirit of the Lord came upon Gideon. He had the anointing of God to cut down the groves and tear down the altars.

My dad used to tell me, "Rex, go out and get the old horse. He has cockleburs in his mane, and they need to be taken out. Now, if you don't want to be kicked or bitten, let me give you some advice: You had better give him a bucket with some oats in it. When he gets his snout down in the bucket and starts eating, you take the currycomb and start pulling out the burs. He will keep on eating, and you can keep on pulling without getting hurt."

If you start pulling and tearing down, but don't have the Spirit of God in you, then you don't have the oats—and brother, you are in trouble. I believe we have a God who can give us the power to take away the trouble, fear, and sin, the cover-ups and the idols that have bound people.

The Bible records: "The Spirit of the Lord came upon Gideon, and he blew a trumpet" (Judges 6:34). Praise God for such a testimony! Gideon's faith in God shone so brightly that his friends and relatives saw that he no longer was "the least in the family." He was a leader—their leader calling them to battle against the Midianites.

My call today is the same as Gideon's. I'm blowing a trumpet, the trumpet of television, radio, and the written word. All across the United States and Canada, I am calling people to repent, to haul down the altars they have built to Baal, and to confess their sins openly before God. When we begin to see that happen, I believe we'll see the beginning of a great revival. Gideon was a failure until he realized there was nothing he could do in his own strength. He had to trust God for the victory.

We must have faith in a God who is able to do the impossible, able to do what we cannot do. Until we believe all things are possible through God, we are working within the framework of man's weakness.

I know that some of you who are reading this are fighting and fussing with your mates. Your children aren't in Sunday school. God isn't honored in the home.

You need to repent of your sins, to get down on your knees and pray. You need to get up and go to church and live for God, to serve Him wherever you are. God will bless you, just as He blessed Gideon, when you turn to Him.

Gideon put his faith to work. He began living a life of action in serving the Lord. You can do the same by praying, giving, and standing together with other people of faith.

If you are running around with every doubter, arguer, and debater you know, you are wasting your time. Get with people who believe in God and His power, with people who believe you can have forgiveness of sins. Get with people who believe in a program of winning souls to Christ.

When Gideon began to act, God began to work, and this farmer—turned soldier for the Lord—saw great victories against impossible odds. He put Satan on the run.

A lot of people are saying, "Well, the devil doesn't bother me." The devil will never bother you as long as you are going in the same direction as he is. But, turn around, and go in the direction of the Lord and you can be sure Satan will be waiting along the side of the road for you.

That's what happened when the Midianites saw that Gideon meant business with the Lord. They brought in an army of 120,000 men and figured to smash Gideon's ragtag bunch to a pulp.

I am sure many people thought Gideon crazy to take 300 men to battle against the tremendous Midianite army. But he trusted in God, not in man. He paid no attention to what people were saying. He received his commands from God, and God gave him a great victory.

The revival I'm believing for is the kind that causes us to repent of our sins, to reinstate our faith in the supernatural God who is able to do anything, to believe God for the impossible and act upon that belief.

A man and his wife in Idaho had been watching our television program every Sunday for two years. One morning they knelt together before the TV set and prayed, "Lord, forgive our sins. We are going to live for you."

They got their children out of bed and went off to a Gospel church where they testified to the saving grace of Jesus Christ. Today, both are Sunday school teachers. God changed two sinners into beautiful instruments to be used for His work.

I lost a couple of listeners that morning, but that is what I am trying to do—get rid of my listeners and send them to Gospel-preaching, soul-saving churches.

There are millions of souls outside of Christ who are just like the enemies of Gideon's day. It didn't take a great army of men to have victory over the Midianites, just a few bound together by their faith in God's power, listening to God and not to man.

If we are to be victorious in the battle against Satan for the control of souls, we must have people who will stand together in their places. We must have people who will believe—who will go into action.

If you need to repent, do it now! Don't thresh your wheat with a defeated attitude. Put your faith in God and He will give you the victory over sin.

Let's have action! Let's read our Bibles daily. Let's pray. Let's go to church and support it with our time, talent, and money.

God is calling you into action. I challenge you to get into a program with me in winning souls for Jesus Christ—whether it is by letter or in person. You know who needs to be told the Gospel story. Let's work together for the Kingdom of God.

If we put our faith into action, God will bless. We could witness unheard-of miracles, and the greatest spiritual awakening the world has ever known!

15

Twentieth Century Paralysis

*And he entered again into the synagogue; and there
was a man there which had a withered hand. And
they watched him, whether he would heal him on
the sabbath day; that they might accuse him. And
he saith unto the man which had the withered hand,
Stand forth. And he saith unto them, Is it lawful to
do good on the sabbath days, or to do evil? To save
life, or to kill? But they held their peace. And when
he had looked round about on them with anger, being
grieved for the hardness of their hearts, he saith unto
the man, Stretch forth thine hand. And he stretched
it out: and his hand was restored whole as the other.*

Mark 3:1–5

In the last chapter we talked about some miracles God wrought
in Old Testament times. Now, here is another miracle—this one
performed by Jesus Himself.

Imagine yourself in Capernaum on that Sabbath day. It was a
special day. People had come to the city from far and near. The
crowd was larger than usual because news had spread that the
new Prophet was going to be in the city.

This was not only a special day, it was a special city, a wonderful city, and Jesus loved it. In fact, we find in the writings of

120

Matthew that Capernaum was called Jesus' own city (Matthew 9:1).

It was here that Jesus performed many mighty works. In Capernaum, He healed the centurion's servant. It was here that Peter's mother-in-law was healed. It was here, also, that the paralytic was healed. It was here that the man who was demon-possessed was delivered. It was in Capernaum that Jesus spoke the words that restored the nobleman's son to health.

Jesus drew great crowds in Capernaum because of His reputation for performing miraculous works. So everyone came—not just those who were seeking the truth, but all of the critics, as well.

The Pharisees were there that day. These men, who were among the respected leaders of the time, were devoted to the Law, and to their religious rituals. They lived disciplined lives. They sacrificed.

This reminds me of a story about an old deacon who was walking down the street one Wednesday evening. One of the church members asked where he was going. He replied, "I'm going to church."

"To church?" the church member asked in shock. "You never attend church on Wednesday night."

"I know, but we're having a business meeting tonight."

"What are you going to vote on?"

"I don't know, but whatever it is, I'm again' it."

Many of the people in Capernaum were just like that, against everything, and especially against this Prophet who was getting so much attention.

But the Pharisees were exclusive and narrow in their beliefs, and severe and hypocritical in their dealings with people. They judged anyone who did not live by their rules. They worshipped according to tradition, and not because they genuinely loved God.

We still have people today who will fellowship with others

only if they agree with them on everything. But this should not be the basis of our fellowship. Our fellowship should be based on Calvary.

The Pharisees forgot that their programs were, for the most part, man-made. There is no Scriptural command for many of the traditions we follow in church. There is no place in the Bible, for instance, where we read that the church should have a choir. There is no place in the Bible where it says to build an altar in the front of the church. There is no place in the Bible where it says there should be ushers. These are man-made contributions.

There is nothing wrong with man's ideas if they are carried out in the spirit of love, and if they exalt Jesus Christ. But when man's programs divide God's people and keep them from meeting God, they are really the devil's programs.

The Pharisees had a lot of forms, fasts and feasts. They had rules for everything—"do this" and "don't do that"—and they believed this was God's will. Now, God could have used this program and wonderfully blessed it, but they had become so narrow and self-righteous that they couldn't even get along with themselves.

When it came to the Sabbath day—brother! They wanted everyone to put on a long face and come down to the synagogue to rehearse a long list of rules and regulations. Their laws were very rigid, and they despised anyone who lived by other principles. Although they had an outward appearance of piety, Jesus knew their hearts, and He saw something that was desperately wrong.

Jesus asked them if it was lawful, in their eyes, to do good on the Sabbath. He wanted to reveal to them that their rigid system of rules was not the way to deal with human need. Jesus' method of dealing with human need was not to open a law book, but to open His heart and stretch out His hand. This man had

a withered hand, and his need could be met only with supernatural power, motivated by love.

How symbolic the man's withered hand is of this generation!
This generation, too, suffers from paralysis—paralysis of the spirit.
People cannot seem to get a firm grip on God and His promises.
They no longer say, "God said it! I believe it! That settles it!"
They want to question the authority of God's Word, to analyze it
instead of just believing it.

Strong hands were a symbol of faith in the Old Testament.
Jacob's strong hands held the angel of the Lord and would not
let go until he had received a blessing. Moses' strong hands held
the rod of authority, and were uplifted in prevailing prayer which
enabled Joshua's men to triumph over Amalek. Samson's strong
hands were mighty in battle against the enemies of God's people.

We need strong hands today! We need Christians who will
pray and work with their hearts, minds, souls, and all their
strength for the glory of God. But, like this man whom Jesus
met in Capernaum, we need to be healed and strengthened by
the supernatural power of God before we can grapple with the
tasks at hand.

How was this man with the withered hand healed? By simply
obeying the command of Jesus! The man had not moved his hand
for many years; it was paralyzed. But when Jesus said to stretch
it out, he did not make excuses, he did not try to postpone what
had to be done. He held out his hand in obedience to the command of Christ, and was healed.

It is time now for the church to be healed, spiritually, by
obediently stretching out and receiving, by faith, the promises
of God. It is time to put our faith into action! Real faith is more
than a general belief in God. The Bible tells us even the devil
believes in God, but that is not saving, delivering faith.

Saving faith includes definite action. According to the Apostle

James, faith without works is dead. Now don't get me wrong—
you can't save yourself by turning over a new leaf, by keeping
the laws of the land, by being a good citizen. You can do all
these things and still be lost if you do not have a Saviour.

But I believe that when Christ comes into a man's life that
man is not going to stick his nose in the devil's trough every
time the slop is poured out. He's going to live for the Lord. If you
say, "I believe in God," live like you really mean it.

If you don't have works with your faith, yours is just a "head
belief" and not a "heart belief," and you need to be born again.
You need to be healed, made new, made whole. Use your strong
hands to get hold of the Bible; read it, study it, believe it and put
it into practice.

Jesus came to Capernaum that day by appointment. He came
not only to bring healing to the man with the withered hand,
but to reveal more of God and His love to the scribes and
Pharisees, to reveal His supernatural power.

I believe that God wants to forgive sin and heal sick and
suffering humanity. I believe He wants to raise up an army of
delivered and dedicated Christians who will be living witnesses
to His grace and power. You can be a part of that army.

Your needs may be obvious, like the need of the man with
the withered hand. Or you may have inner needs that are easily
covered over, so that other people are not aware of your incom-
pleteness—your shortcomings. But Jesus knows your needs. He
knew the inner need of the Pharisees, and would have healed
them, too, if they had acknowledged that need and turned to
Him in faith.

The Lord sees you now and knows your need. He knows your
name and address. He knows your future, and when you are
going to die. He knows every thought that is going through your
mind right now.

Can you maintain a bold outward appearance when you know

that Christ can see inside of you? You may need to take an inward look. A cover-up of self-righteousness will not save you; our righteousness is as filthy rags, according to the Word of God.

There are two classes of needy people, just as there were in Capernaum so long ago: those who have a need and present themselves to Jesus for saving, healing and restoration; and those who try to cover up their spiritual needs with superficial rituals and spiritual activity.

To the first group Jesus says, "Stretch forth your hand and be made whole." For the other group there are no words of comfort; they will cover up their withered hands and go out without their needs being met.

Which group are you in now?

I hope you will be in that number who will confess their needs. The healing hands of Jesus are reaching out to you now. Whatever your need, no matter how great your problem, reach out to Him—and do it now.

16

After Six Days

And after six days Jesus taketh Peter, James, and John his brother, and bringeth them up into an high mountain apart. And was transfigured before them: and his face did shine as the sun, and his raiment was white as the light. And, behold, there appeared unto them Moses and Elias talking with him. Then answered Peter, and said unto Jesus, Lord, it is good for us to be here: if thou wilt, let us make here three tabernacles; one for thee, and one for Moses, and one for Elias. While he yet spake, behold, a bright cloud overshadowed them: and behold a voice out of the cloud, which said, This is my beloved Son, in whom I am well pleased; hear ye him. And when the disciples heard it, they fell on their face, and were sore afraid. And Jesus came and touched them, and said, Arise, and be not afraid. And when they had lifted up their eyes, they saw no man, save Jesus only.

Matthew 17:1–8

As the end of his stay on earth drew near, Jesus knew that He must prepare His disciples to carry on His work when He was gone. One day, He asked them an all-important question: "Whom say ye that I am?" In reply, Peter came up with that memorable declaration, "Thou art the Christ, the Son of the living God."

126

Then Jesus told them that upon that confession He would build His Church ". . . and the gates of hell shall not prevail against it" (Matthew 16:15–18).

Now, someone will say, "That is our denomination; we have built it on Peter." But Jesus didn't mean that His Church would be built on Peter, himself; He referred to Peter's confession that Jesus was the Christ. And to this day any life that is built on that, and any church that is built on that, is going to stand, just as surely as anything that is not built on Christ, the Son of the living God, is going to fall.

And let me tell you something—no matter what your denomination is, it has split more than once, and the gates of hell *have* prevailed against it. The gates of hell have prevailed against every earthly man's organization. But there is one Church, the Church of the living God, that the gates of hell have never prevailed against, and never will. The only way you can get into this Church is by being born again. Every man, woman, boy or girl that has confessed his or her sins and accepted the atonement of Calvary is in the Church of the living God, whether he or she has a dark skin, a yellow skin, or a red skin.

Man has taken it upon himself and made this denomination and that denomination. But before the rapture of the Church there is going to come a day when you will see JESUS ONLY—not a tabernacle for Elias, not a tabernacle for Moses, not a tabernacle for the Methodists, the Baptists, the Presbyterians, or the Humbardites. God's people are going to have a revival that will spread throughout the world. There will be a great salvation of souls before the Lord's return. I believe this with all my heart.

"Thou art the Christ, the Son of the living God." Peter was ready to confess it. Then Jesus went on to tell them about His death for the sins of men, and that His time was short. He explained that He had come to do the will of His Father—that He was born to die. "Then Peter took him, and began to rebuke him, saying, Be it far from thee, Lord: this shall not be unto thee. But he turned, and said unto Peter, Get thee behind me, Satan (Matthew 16:22, 23). He did not mean by that that Peter was Satan, but that Satan had put those words into Peter's mouth.

One day, when Jesus was travelling with His disciples, a man named Jairus came looking for Him. Jairus' only daughter was dying, and he wanted Jesus to come and save her life. Now Jairus was a very important man, a ruler of the synagogue. What prestige to go to his house and heal his daughter! But as Jesus was hurrying toward Jairus' house someone in the crowd touched His garment—someone the doctors had tried to heal and failed. She had tried many physicians, and had spent all that she had. Then she heard about the Lord and said, "If I may but touch his garment, I shall be whole" (Matthew 9:21). When Jesus felt the tips of her fingers touch the hem of His garment, He stopped. He did not say, "Come on, boys, the revival is going on down the road at Jairus' house." He said, "Who touched me?" His disciples pointed out that everybody was bumping into Him. But Jesus knew that this was a different touch, and the woman was healed instantly.

When we touch Jesus everything is changed. The blind are made to see, the lame walk, the deaf hear, and the dumb speak.

As Jesus continued on to Jairus' house, someone came running up and said that the daughter was dead. I can just see the poor man as sorrow clutched his heart, but the Lord turned to him and said, "Be not afraid, only believe" (Mark 5:36). They walked on to the house, and a great throng was gathered. In those days they had paid mourners. They were moaning and groaning, and the Lord walked in and said, "Why make ye this ado, and weep? the damsel is not dead, but sleepeth" (Mark 5:39). And they laughed Him to scorn. Then Jesus told them all to get out. Only the inner circle was to remain—only those who had faith. And

He took with Him Peter, James, and John and went in and raised the dead.

Now, let us look at these three who belonged to Jesus' inner circle.

Peter was full of energy and zeal. You remember that when they were having the Lord's Supper and Jesus told Peter that he would deny Him, Peter jumped up and said, "Though I should die with thee, yet will I not deny thee" (Matthew 26:35). That's what I like about Peter: Do something, even if you do the wrong thing. Please do something; don't just sit around and be afraid you will make a mistake. I would rather see someone make ten mistakes and do one thing right than not do anything at all.

John was the beloved disciple. I can just see John as they bring in someone who is sick with the palsy, or someone who cannot walk, or is blind, or a leper. He begins to wipe the tears from his eyes; he is touched with the feeling of their infirmities. John was the one who, the Bible tells us, laid his head on the Lord's breast. It was clear that he loved Him. And I want to tell you, my friend, if you want Jesus to help you, you must love Him, too. Your life may be full of pain and problems, but you can praise your Lord anyway. Even if pain is going all through your body, praise God, and you'll find out that He will never fail you.

The third disciple, John's brother James, was a martyr of the Church; he was one of those who died for the cause of Christ.

Jesus wanted these three with Him because He knew they believed in Him. Give me a church full of people that have faith, and I will show you a church where people will be saved, and people will be healed. With faith, all things are possible. Your faith—or lack of it—can either bless or hinder the church's service. So have faith in God—only believe.

I say that the services we are carrying on in our churches today are so far from the will of God that God cannot bless, God cannot meet our needs, He cannot save our souls and He cannot heal our bodies because we preachers have come to a place where we think we have to sing three songs, take the offering, preach twelve minutes, and then go home. Any time Jesus had a meeting, it wasn't three songs and a twelve-minute essay. At times He went out and preached all day long. And while He was preaching He opened blind eyes, unstopped deaf ears, and made the lame to walk. It was an all-day revival.

I wish the Lord would pour out blessings in our church services so we would not be able to go home until daylight. That would be the will of the Lord. If at any time during a service we feel we want to stop preaching and give the altar call, that is what we ought to do. I could go on and say, "Now we have a planned program. We have a guest here, and what will he think?" Brother, I don't care what he thinks. I don't care what anyone thinks. All I want to know is—Lord, what do *You* want? And whatever is His will, I pray that He will help me be obedient to His voice. As many as are led by the Lord are the sons of God.

Do you remember a time when God spoke to your heart to pray but you went on about your work, and after awhile the burden lifted? Brother or sister, if you go on with your work and that burden lifts, when you go into your room to pray you are fighting against the wall. We say, "O God" and it bounces right back in our face, and it ought to bounce. Whatever you are doing when God calls you to pray, stop and get down on your knees, and the glory will hit your soul.

God speaks to you about getting back, Backslider, and you say, "Not now, but sometime I'm going to get right with God." When that sometime comes you will find that the Spirit is not there, and when you pray you are going to wonder why you can't get the victory. What you ought to do is listen to God when He speaks. Then you will get the victory. "No man can come to me, except the Father which hath sent me draw him" (John 6:44).

It was Jesus' three chosen disciples—Peter, James, and John—

that He took up to the Mount of Transfiguration. Why did He do it? It was for a divine revelation. That divine revelation was not to erect a church for Moses and the Law; it was not to erect a church for Elias and the Prophets; but for the One whom Moses and the Prophets wrote about—Jesus of Nazareth, the Son of the living God, the promised Messiah. Now the Lord is in the valley, as well as on the mountaintop: "Yea, though I walk through the valley of the shadow of death, I will fear no evil: for thou art with me; thy rod and thy staff they comfort me" (Psalms 23:4). Do you believe the Lord will be down in the valley? I do. But He will be down in the valley to lift you up. He will be down in the valley to encourage you.

But do you know where you get your divine revelation and your vision and your prophecy and your dreams? Not in the valley, but on the mountaintop.

This is the day of the Lord, this is the greatest age the world has ever known. It is the Holy Ghost dispensation. The Kingdom of Heaven is at hand. This is what Christ preached. The divine revelation was that Moses and Elias were there. That means, first of all, that we will live after this life. Then they disappeared and they saw no man save JESUS ONLY.

Jesus is not going to take everyone into His Kingdom. (There were twelve disciples, but He took only three.) He is not going to take every Tom, Dick, and Harry, that has never accepted Him. This great revival that is going to break out before the rapture of the Church, is not going to include a lot of people with sinful habits in their lives, either. Not a bunch of carnal Christians, nor backsliding preachers, it will be those who are in the inner circle; those who are full of zeal and energy and already doing something for God. God is not going around picking up people who are not busy. He is going to take some poor little country plowboy who is preaching up a storm down in the hills of Arkansas and setting the woods on fire. He is going to take godly mothers and grandmothers who have been praying for years that God would bless the Church.

God is going to take those who will sympathize with the sick, the suffering, the sinners, and those who are dying. Where is He going to take them? Not to a valley, but to a mountaintop—for a divine revelation. What will that divine revelation be in the last days? That divine revelation will be that it will not be the Methodists, Baptists, Presbyterians, Pentecostals or Holiness, but the Lord Jesus Christ and Him only, crucified. Then God will take them into the inner circle and they will catch a glimpse of Jesus—the only thing that will make the Church ready for the rapture, a Church without spot, without wrinkle, without blemish. The Church today has a spot; it has hatred, it has bad habits, it has backbiting, it has fighting among the believers of Christ, it has politics, and everything else.

In that day—the last of six days—first of all, God is going to send a revival. It is the only thing that will get the Church ready. "And it shall come to pass afterward, that I will pour out my spirit upon all flesh" (Joel 2:28). On the day of Pentecost was the beginning of that pouring out. Three thousand people were saved that one day. That was the BEGINNING of the last days and this is the CLOSING of the last days.

The Lord said they would wax worse and worse until the end, deceiving and being deceived. That is right, but that is not God's Church He is talking about. That is the people with a form without the Power. (In the last days there are people who will have a form of godliness and deny the Power.) According to the Bible, in the last days children will be disobedient to parents, but that does not mean that Christians are to sit around and let their children run all over them. Bless your heart, you are supposed to take care of your children.

Let's get this straight, the WORLD will wax worse and worse until the end, with people deceiving and being deceived. The form of godliness will be more of a form, and more of a form denying the Power. We have it today: They have torn "Power in the Blood" out of the song book. They call it "slaughterhouse religion."

They have churches today you can join over the telephone, and send your picture in to be baptized. You are a full-fledged member if you will just pay your dues every month. I don't like to talk about the preachers, but some of them need to be talked about. They should not be preaching the Gospel; God never called them to preach. They need to be born again. If the blind lead the blind, they will both fall in the ditch. Now, that crowd is going to wax worse and worse until the end, deceiving and being deceived. But the Bible does NOT say that the born-again Christian is going to wax worse and worse.

The Lord said in His Word that He is coming for a Church without spot, without wrinkle and without blemish. Now, this is the way I think it is all going to come about: I think that GOD IS NOW CALLING OUT PEOPLE OF ALL DENOMINATIONS. It is happening in Akron, it is happening in Los Angeles, it is happening in Dallas, it is happening around the world. A REVIVAL IS BREAKING OUT AMONG CHRISTIANS. And this time it is not a revival in any denomination. It is not a revival led by a bunch of well-known preachers.

Then after six days, at the close of six thousand years, the Lord is going to take up those who will pay the price, up onto that Mount of Transfiguration, and the Lord is going to be revealed. It is not going to be the denomination, but it is going to be "Christ in us, the hope of glory."

No longer will the Body of Christ be divided, but WE WILL BE ONE, and the Power is going to be poured out upon us. You will be able to walk down the street, as a Christian, and say to a little boy sitting along the way with twisted limbs, "Silver and gold have I none, but in the name of Jesus rise up and walk." Every born-again Christian who pays the price is going to be given the Power.

There is going to be such a great revival that we are going to forget our denomination. We are going to see JESUS ONLY—and right in the middle of this revival, God is going to send His Son back for His Church.

17

Will the United States Fight in World War III?

But of that day and hour knoweth no man, no, not the angels of heaven, but my Father only. But as the days of Noe were, so shall also the coming of the Son of man be. For as in the days that were before the flood they were eating and drinking, marrying and giving in marriage, until the day that Noe entered into the ark, And knew not until the flood came, and took them all away; so shall also the coming of the Son of man be. Matthew 24:36–39

Certainly, when we list the Scriptures which refer to the return of Jesus Christ, we have to include Matthew, Chapter 24. I would have you note also 2 Chronicles 16:7–9 and 17:6–10. And we must remember to read still another Old Testament book, Ezekiel, because Ezekiel had so much to say about this. I suggest the reading begin at Chapter 25 and continue on through Ezekiel, Chapters 37, 38 and 39. In addition, it might be helpful to go back and read the little Book of Joel.

Now, where do we stand in God's time clock? All of us know that this time clock has been guided by prophecy. One of the important indicators that all Biblical scholars look to is the re-establishing of the nation of Israel. Long before this ever took place, God prophesied in His Word that, because of their rejection of His Son, Jesus Christ, the Jewish people would be scattered throughout all the nations of the world. Christ was a Jew, but because of their rebellion, their sin, and the Jews' rejection of Christ as God's Son, the period of the Holy Ghost dispensation was ushered in. Through this dispensation, whosoever will may come. All nationalities, all people everywhere can be saved by placing their trust in Christ.

There was a time, in the Old Testament, when God dealt directly with man. There was the flood in which, because of wickedness and sin, God destroyed all except Noah and his family. God had been long-suffering, however, for though He pronounced judgment, Noah worked and God waited for 120 years before the flood waters finally came. Don't forget that. In God's time clock, we do not know the day or the hour, but we know the event.

We must realize that God sends judgment because of rejection and sin. If we would repent of our sins, God would reduce judgment. This is illustrated in the events which took place in Nineveh. Jonah went down and preached to Nineveh, and they repented, and because of this God spared Nineveh. Judgment comes because of sin. Removal of God's judgment occurs only through repentance; and everyone who is a sinner today is pronounced under a judgment of hell and banishment from God forever in eternity. The judgment of God is lifted only if one repents and is saved.

We know that God's Word does say that in the end of the Church Age, when Jesus shall return, these times shall be revealed unto us. In the days of Noah, the people were eating and drinking and marrying and giving in marriage and knew not until the flood came. (See Matthew 24:37–39; Luke 17:25–30.) There shall be wars and rumors of wars in these days, and so shall it be in the days before the coming of God's Son.

One of the truths which the Bible plainly teaches is the re-establishing of Israel after 2000 years of being scattered throughout the nations of the world. There were 2000 years until the time of the flood, 2000 years from the flood until the coming of Christ and the fulfillment of that prophecy; and now almost 2000 years have passed since then.

In the Gospel of Matthew, the Bible says that because flesh was so wicked, because man was so wicked and the power in his hand was so that he would destroy himself off the face of the earth, God had to cut short the time. "And except those days should be shortened, there should no flesh be saved: but for the elect's sake those days shall be shortened" (Matthew 24:22). This Holy Ghost dispensation will not live out its 2000 years. God will cut it short. How short? Perhaps one hour, one year, two years—how short, we do not know. But I do know this: The signs of the times are at hand, and the next great event to take place is the return of Jesus Christ. The Bible says, in the same chapter of Matthew in which He said the time would be short, that this generation should not pass till all be fulfilled (Matthew 24:34–36).

(A generation is usually considered to be about a third of a century, or in other words, the earthly life span of Jesus Christ, which was 33 and one-half years. The fig tree is symbolic of the budding nation of Israel, which is now regathered into her land and has been recognized, since May 1948, as a nation—for the first time in 2500 years.)

This generation is rapidly expiring. Time is running out! No man knows the day or the hour, not even Christ, but the Father only; but be assured that the time is at hand.

Christ is coming back to catch away the Church. Who is the Church? Someone will say those with some special gift, or members of a certain denomination, but the Bible says the

Church is the people who have been born again by the Spirit of God, of all denominations, and all faiths, those who have a personal knowledge of Christ as their Saviour, with the Spirit of Christ dwelling within them (Romans 8:9).

All will be called away, whether Methodists, Baptists, Presbyterians, Nazarenes, or Pentecostals—all of these and the rest who know Jesus Christ. It might be compared to taking a magnet and placing it against match sticks; they won't move. But take the magnet and place it against metal pins or nails, and they catch on! So, everyone who has been born again of the Spirit and baptized into the Body of Christ is going to be called away when the Lord comes. If you are a believer in Jesus Christ, your body is the temple of the Holy Ghost, and when you are caught away, the Spirit will respond to God's call.

What is to take place then? There will be the establishment of the Antichrist. The world is leading up to a world federation of churches. It is laying aside belief in the authority and divine inspiration of the Word of God, and in supernatural events such as the virgin birth. Man is making his own book of laws and rules and regulations. If anyone or anything asserts that, "I am Christ," but denies the real Christ, he is anti-Christ. There will soon be a world religion, according to God's Word. (See Revelation, Chapter 13 and 2 Thessalonians, Chapter 2.)

Now, in the Book of Revelation, it says that the Antichrist will appear and there will also be a world dictator. These two will unite—the religious and the political forces. If we took the federation of all the religions which deny the supernatural and united them, we would have a world control power and a world religious power. You say it will never happen? Well, people are tired of war, people are tired of strife, people are tired of poverty, and the Antichrist preaches and advocates peace, safety, security, and plenty. This will be the situation for three and one-half years. Then, it shall follow that every man shall have a mark in his head, the mark of the beast. (See Revelation 13:16–18.)

The Antichrist, of whom we now speak, is a total dictator—political, economic and religious—who will arise out of a restored Roman Empire and be identified with it. (See Revelation 17:8–18.) Four great Gentile empires of world proportion—Babylon, Media-Persia, Greece and Rome—have already dominated throughout the centuries. These empires are typified in the mind of man by a great image (see Daniel 2:31–43), but in the mind of God they are typified by four great beasts. (See Daniel, Chapter 17.) The prophet Daniel gave special consideration to the fourth beast. (See Daniel 7:19–28 and compare with Matthew 24:27–30, 25:31–34; Revelation 19:11–21.)

God revealed also to Daniel the Kingdom of God which should follow the four Gentile kingdoms. (See Daniel 2:44–45, 7:9–14.) The Son of Man (Jesus Christ) will be given dominion and glory, and a Kingdom that all people and nations should serve. His dominion is everlasting, and shall not pass away, and His Kingdom is that which shall not be destroyed.

In the Book of Daniel, God indicates His people, Israel, as the "time clock" by which we may know God's plan of events for the ages. (See Acts 15:14–18.) Read Daniel 9:24–27 to understand the 70 weeks of years relating to Israel; that is, seven years to each week, or a total of 490 years. In the first seven weeks, or 49 years, Jerusalem was to be rebuilt. Sixty-two weeks later (434 years after the temple was rebuilt), the Messiah was to come. Israel's chastisement, as recorded in Deuteronomy, Chapter 28, could have been ended at this time had she been converted to her Messiah, but Israel rejected Christ at the end of the 69th week. The 70th week is yet to be reckoned upon Israel, at Christ's Second Coming. Her conversion to Christ will take place during these seven years. During the interval of time between Israel's rejection of her Messiah (almost 2000 years ago) and now, the church (the Gentile Bride of Christ) is being formed. The 70th week of Daniel (7 years) is now almost ready to begin. It will be divided into two periods of three and one-half years each.

Arising on the scene during the first of these periods will be the Antichrist, whom the world will regard as her protector. Israel will fear Russia, and will look to the Antichrist as her saviour from Russia. Ezekiel, Chapters 36–39, tells us of Russia's doom. Russia will be cursed of God for her move against Israel. The Antichrist will take credit for Russia's defeat, and will set himself up as God and demand worship of both Jew and Gentile. (See 2 Thessalonians 2:3–4.) No one shall be able to buy or sell without his approval (Revelation 13:17).

I feel that today, through our own government, as well as other governments of the world, everybody is becoming a number. Man will be known by a number in his forehead, and I think you will have to memorize that number so you can repeat it if they ask you who you are. To buy or sell, or to do anything, you will have to have a number. The Bible says, "in your forehead." I don't think they're going to tattoo it on your forehead; I think you're going to have to memorize it. Today, if someone were to ask me my name, I would say, "I am Rex Humbard." It's not tattooed on me; it's in my forehead, in my brain. I believe you're going to have to memorize your Social Security number someday, as you do your name, and that's the way you're going to live. You are going to be a number. That is what the Bible says (Revelation 13:17).

After three and one-half years, the alliance between Israel and the Antichrist and the mark of the beast will be broken, and then the bloodiest battle in the history of the world will be fought. If you will read in the Old Testament, in Ezekiel, it says the northern power (and many Bible scholars agree that the northern power is Russia) will march south, down through

Syria, upon Palestine and in that moment and hour God Almighty will turn the heavens and the elements into fire, brimstone and hail, and the armies of Russia will be defeated by God Almighty, not by man. And great things will take place: The fish in the sea will die, the mountains will be brought low, men and women, boys and girls will be killed—we will witness a battle such as the world has never known (Revelation 8:7-13). The fighting will continue until the blood will reach the bridle bits of the horses (Revelation 14:20). Israel will know the way of the Lord, whom they rejected, and who hung upon the cross, and they will receive Jesus Christ (Zechariah 12:10, 13:6). Then Israel will become the world's missionary to preach Christ.

When the trouble has subsided and the northern powers of Russia are defeated by God Almighty and His armies (Ezekiel, Chapters 36-39), there will be a great rejoicing in the Lord and a great outpouring of God's Spirit upon Israel. The Holy Ghost dispensation will be closed, of course, because Jesus will already have come and caught His Church away. (See Luke 21:36; 1 Thessalonians 5:1-6; Revelation 3:10.) Now a new church, a new nation, will be born unto the Lord, to become the missionaries of the world. (See Revelation 7:4-17, 11:1-22, 12:11.)

God will be greatly grieved, for it will take over seven months to bury the dead (Ezekiel 39:11), and there will be graves all over the hillsides of Israel. Men will try to get the dead buried; yet everywhere they go, they will see bodies, and they will put up signs until someone will come and bury the dead (Ezekiel 39:15). God will call the eagles and vultures and other birds, and He will say, "Come and eat the flesh of the kings and rulers and great men; they have been destroyed" (Ezekiel 39:17-20).

Then, Jesus is coming back. He is coming back to set up an earthly kingdom. For one thousand years He will reign upon the earth. (See Revelation 20:4.) The lions and the lambs will lie down together (Isaiah 11:6-9); and there will be no war any more. There will be peace and happiness and joy, for God will have established a Kingdom where Christ is the ruler and the devil will have been defeated. (See Isaiah 2:4; Micah 4:3.) God's plan will be fulfilled, and the capital city of heaven will float right down here, and people who have been redeemed and are with the Lord will return (Revelation 21:2). Those who have gone away are going to come back. (See 2 Timothy 2:11–12; Revelation 20:4.) There won't be any pain or heartache or troubles (Revelation 7:17, 21:4). Bless God, someday I expect to walk out of the gate of heaven and come back and visit Akron. Jesus will reign for one thousand years, and I expect to be in the number of the redeemed.

War is the direct curse upon the human race, because of our rebellion against God and the principles of God, people have turned down God, and His ways (James 4:1–10).

What brought on war in the Old Testament? It was because people went their own way, lived in sin, and forgot God, that God allowed war, calamity, and destruction to come (Deuteronomy 28:15–68). Calamity fell on the wicked and the ungodly, but when the people repented and asked God for forgiveness, then God placed in their hands peace, and brought fear to the nations of the world who bothered them. (See Deuteronomy 28:10; the Book of Judges; 2 Chronicles 17:10.)

In the Old Testament, 2 Chronicles, it has been recorded in Chapter 16:7: "Because thou hast relied on the king of Syria, and not relied on the Lord thy God, therefore is the host of the king of Syria escaped out of thine hand." God said they had done foolishly, and therefore from that time forth they should have wars. Now, King Asa was a great man, a man of God; he was a man after God's own heart, who ruled ten centuries before Christ came into the world. He tore down the heathen gods and the altars the people had erected unto heathen gods. He furnished the temple of the true and living God—furnished it properly and rightly. When Asa's own mother, who was a queen, began to serve idols and false gods, he even took her out and had her destroyed because she had forsaken the true and living God, and had tried to lead the people away.

However, when the enemies of the North looked down and said, "Let's go down to the people of the Lord and make them our prey, these people of faith who trust in the Lord!" we find that fear gripped the heart of King Asa, and in this hour of fear he did not call a prayer meeting, he did not call upon the people of God, or upon a servant of God. Instead, he made three mistakes. The first was that he relied, not on the Lord, but on human hands. He was guilty of going out and making alliances with nations that had false gods and idols. (See 2 Chronicles, Chapter 16.) This was Asa's mistake, and God pronounced war to come upon him because he made alliances with the ungodly and no longer feared the Lord. (See 2 Chronicles 16:12.)

If I read my history right, the United States of America went into an alliance with an ungodly nation that killed 30 million Christians, one which says there is no God. Unless we repent, destruction is ours; we have made alliances with the ungodly. After 2000 years, God's people today need a revival and a return to the Lord.

Now, not only did Asa refuse to rely on God, and make alliances, but what else did he do? He went to the house of the Lord because he needed money, and he took the money from the people of God, and from God's house. He took the silver and gold and gave it to the heathens as a bribe for their alliances. (See 1 Kings 15:18.) I can read to you from the pages of my history book how the United States has taxed the people. Christians haven't given to God their tenth, we haven't served the Lord as we should, but the United States has taxed her people, only to run this country into debt billions of dollars. Because it has given to the ungodly, who in turn have burned our flag, spit in our ambassadors' faces, and made fun of our God, there will be punishment.

I have traveled a little bit in the last few years, and I noticed when I was in Syria that I rode on highways paid for by our tax dollars. I rode on highways in Cairo, Egypt, which were built by our tax dollars. I went to Jordan and rode on highways made possible by our tax dollars. I went to Israel and rode on highways paid for by our tax dollars. When we think of all the war and destruction and evil, there has to be some repenting in America. We have made fun of God; we have run Him out of our schools; we have thrown Him out of our Supreme Court; we have thrown Him out of our lives. Those in Congress need to get on their knees and call a prayer meeting, and we preachers should back it. But I'll say something more—my heart breaks when I ask, "Where are the ministers of America today?" We are out doing other things instead of getting on our knees and calling upon God.

Asa took what belonged to God and gave to the enemies of God, and God was displeased with him and told him that his nation would have war, trouble, and strife, all because of it. Refusing to rely on God, making alliances with the enemies of God— these were two things, but the third thing he did was to rob God.

What's wrong with the world? What's wrong with the people who call themselves people of faith? I'll tell you what's wrong: they've sinned—they've forgotten God, and destruction lies ahead. No, America will not *have* to fight in World War III. American boys *could* be spared from having their blood shed in the Battle of Armageddon, but only if we'll do what the son of Asa did.

You see, Asa disobeyed God, and God was displeased and let him die. Then Jehoshaphat, his son, inherited the throne. But Jehoshaphat went back and broke off the alliance with the ungodly.

(See 2 Chronicles, Chapter 17.) He gave back to the church the wealth and power and authority. He told the ministers to go up and down the land proclaiming the Word of God. He called the families together and demanded that fathers and mothers teach in their homes the ways of the Lord, that they live for God and trust in Him. This is what King Jehoshaphat did, and then what did God Almighty do? God recorded it here in 2 Chronicles 17:6 and 10: "And his heart was lifted up in the ways of the Lord: . . . And the fear of the Lord fell upon all the kingdoms of the lands that were round about Judah, so that they made no war against Jehoshaphat."

There was war and destruction because of disobedience, and there was peace and safety because of obedience. I believe the coming world conflict will be the most destructive war the world has ever known. I believe that America can be spared if America will repent and get right with God. But, if we don't have revival, we will be caught up in this terrible, devastating conflict.

18

The Absolute Certainty of Jesus' Coming Again

Let not your heart be troubled: ye believe in God, believe also in me. In my Father's house are many mansions: if it were not so, I would have told you. I go to prepare a place for you. And if I go and prepare a place for you, I will come again, and receive you unto myself; that where I am, there ye may be also. And whither I go ye know, and the way ye know. Thomas saith unto him, Lord, we know not whither thou goest; and how can we know the way? Jesus saith unto him, I am the way, and the truth, and the life: no man cometh unto the Father, but by me.

John 14:1–6

"Yet a little while, and he that shall come will come, and will not tarry." This is the positive declaration of the Holy Spirit, as recorded in Hebrews 10:37. It leaves no room for doubting the fact that Jesus will certainly come back again. No subject has undergone more attacks, more perversions and subversions since Satan first assailed the divine inspiration of the Holy Scriptures and the deity of Christ. Many conflicting views and beliefs have been filling the air in recent years, until the Christian doesn't know now what to believe about Jesus' coming. Preachers are hesitant

146

to preach on this important subject for fear conflicting views will bring divisions in their churches or denominations. And Satan couldn't be happier, as he is the author of all this confusion, and it is in his master plan of strategy to nullify the relevance of Jesus' return to the church of our day.

Why does the devil hate this message of the certainty of Jesus' coming? First of all, because it is the purifying hope of every born-again Christian. "And every man that hath this hope in him purifieth himself, even as he [Jesus] is pure" (1 John 3:3). If we can be cheated out of the certainty of this precious truth, then the enemy of our souls can disarm us from being ready for our Saviour's coming. Frequently, Jesus cautioned us to be ready: "Therefore be ye also ready: for in such an hour [not day, month or year] as ye think not the Son of man cometh" (Matthew 24:44). In this very same chapter, you do not have to read more than four verses further before finding a lukewarm, backsliding servant of God braying the devil's doctrine: "My Lord delayeth his coming."

You see, he did not believe Jesus could come in this generation. He believed, as some are advocating even now, that Jesus cannot come until the middle of the Tribulation; others insist that He will not come until the end of the Great Tribulation; some say, He came at Pentecost; while still others believe He comes when we are saved from our sins. In contrast to the Bible's teaching, another group even believes Jesus comes again when we die, and that He takes us up to Heaven. All of these confusing, false beliefs are right now being propagated among fundamental churches in America.

But much more serious than these errors are the sneering remarks from those who have gone into apostasy. They sarcastically protest: "We have heard that stuff from the time we were little children, but it hasn't happened yet." Let me assure you, it will take place just as Jesus, the angels, the apostles and the Holy Spirit declare in the Bible!

Paul wrote, in Romans 13:11–13, "And that, knowing the time, that now it is high time to awake out of sleep: for now is our salvation nearer than when we believed. The night is far spent, the day is at hand: let us therefore cast off the works of darkness, and let us put on the armour of light. Let us walk honestly, as in the day; not in rioting and drunkenness, not in chambering and wantonness, not in strife and envying."

And in 1 John 2:28 we read, "And now, little children, abide in him; that, when he shall appear, we may have confidence, and not be ashamed before him at his coming."

This is the key verse that unlocks all the enemies' attacks on the subject about the certainty of Jesus' coming. Satan wants all of us to be unprepared and not ready for Jesus, for he knows, far better than most ministers do, what Jesus said in Matthew 25:10: ". . . The bridegroom came; and they that were ready went in with him to the marriage: and the door was shut."

In Revelation 19:7 we see a scene in heaven and hear these words: "Let us be glad and rejoice, and give honour to him: for the marriage of the Lamb is come, and his wife [the Church] hath made herself ready."

No true minister or Bible teacher can rightly divide the word of truth without seeing the serious implications which are involved in this term "ready" and the stern warnings which our precious Lord gave so frequently. On one occasion Jesus spoke these words: "Be ye therefore ready also: for the Son of man cometh at an hour when ye think not" (Luke 12:40). When the apostle questioned Him about this admonition, Jesus gave this answer: "And what I say unto you I say unto all, Watch" (Mark 13:37).

Our wonderful Lord would never tell us to be ready, to watch, to wait, or to look for His coming if He never intended to come again. He would never lie to us or deceive us into thinking He could come just any minute, if such were not the case. All of these words—*watch, look, be ready, wait*—denote momentary expectancy. They are the kind of positive exhortations found in all the New Testament writings on Jesus' coming.

The Holy Spirit would not diminish the importance of this vital truth by underemphasis. Over 287 references to the coming of our Lord Jesus are found in the New Testament alone. This fact, in itself, ought to stir every true and faithful believer, every preacher or teacher of the Lord's Word who has this same Holy Spirit within him. Surely we ought to feel the same way about Jesus' coming as the Holy Spirit does.

There is a great spirit of revival moving across the country. Accompanying it is a revival of the declaration of Jesus' certain return. This revival would have to happen just prior to His coming, else there would be no reason for the scoffers which are to come in the last days to ridicule this second-coming message. If it were a dead doctrine, long since abandoned as untrue and forgotten, we should just stop talking about it.

The apostle Peter speaks of these false deceivers in this manner: "Knowing this first, that there shall come in the last days scoffers, walking after their own lusts, And saying, Where is the promise of his coming? for since the fathers fell asleep, all things continue as they were from the beginning of the creation" (2 Peter 3:3, 4). Peter brands this reasoning as willful ignorance. There are too many facts and details and repetitions of this glorious truth to escape any honest heart.

Jesus said: "I go to prepare a place for you. And if I go and prepare a place for you, I will come again, and receive you unto myself; that where I am, there ye may be also" (John 14:2, 3).

Peter encouraged the believers with these words: "The trial of your faith, being much more precious than of gold that perisheth, though it be tried with fire, might be found unto praise and honour and glory at the appearing of Jesus Christ" (1 Peter 1:7). "Wherefore gird up the loins of your mind, be sober, and hope to the end for the grace that is to be brought unto you at the revelation of Jesus Christ" (1 Peter 1:13). "And He shall send Jesus Christ, which before was preached unto you" (Acts 3:20).

Beloved, the Lord's "shalls" mean *shall.* There is no room for "hope so," "guess so," "maybe," or "perhaps," for in Hebrews 9:28, we read: "So Christ was once offered to bear the sins of many; and unto them that look for him shall he appear the second time without sin unto salvation," and in 1 Thessalonians 4:16, 17: "For the Lord himself shall descend from heaven with a shout, with the voice of the archangel, and with the trump of God: and the dead in Christ shall rise first: Then we which are alive and remain shall be caught up together with them in the clouds, to meet the Lord in the air: and so shall we ever be with the Lord."

I remember reading in Luke 2:25–35 of a dear old saint named Simeon. It was revealed to him by the same Spirit of God that he would not die until he had seen the Redeemer of the world, our Messiah. Even then, there were those around him who thought he was a "little off upstairs" or "had rooms for rent in his upper story." But, to their utter surprise, that elderly saint kept living on and on, although many expected him to die just any day. He openly affirmed the fact that he couldn't die until he had seen Jesus in His first coming. If God could reveal the first coming of Jesus to certain ones who were living close to His heart, then I affirm that He is able to do the same today regarding Jesus' second coming.

Jesus told us seven times in Revelation, chapters two and three, to hear what the Spirit is saying to the churches. The Spirit must be speaking, for Jesus tells us to listen. In the concluding chapter of this wonderful book, Jesus speaks this thrilling message (Chapter 22 verse 7): "Behold, I come quickly: blessed is he that keepeth the sayings of the prophecy of this book." Then, in verse 12: "And, behold, I come quickly; and my reward is with me, to give every man according as his work shall be." And finally, in verse 20: "He which testifieth these things saith, Surely I come quickly. Amen."

The glad response which came from the writer of this last book of the Bible was: "Even so, come, Lord Jesus." This is also our hearty response and earnest prayer when we are ready and really saved, and eager to meet Him. Jesus loved us, and gave Himself for us on the cross to purchase our lost souls. We are now "Looking for that blessed hope, and the glorious appearing of the great God and our Saviour Jesus Christ; Who gave himself for us, that he might redeem us from all iniquity, and purify unto himself a peculiar people, zealous of good works" (Titus 2:13–15).

Our looking is not in vain in the least. Manifold signs which Jesus and the apostles prophesied concerning His coming are being fulfilled before our very eyes, showing that the time is near for our Lord to come back. One very important one is found in 2 Timothy 3:1, 2: "This know also, that in the last days perilous times shall come. For men shall be lovers of their own selves. . . ."

Jesus will return on time, just as He did the first time, as declared in Galatians 4:4, 5: "But when the fulness of time was come, God sent forth his Son, made of a woman, made under the law, To redeem them that were under the law, that we might receive the adoption of sons." God's great prophetic clock is ticking away the hours, and soon an unprepared and amazed world will awaken to the fulfillment of Jesus' sudden coming and the catching away of His waiting Bride, the Church.

Jesus said: "Watch ye therefore, and pray always, that ye may be accounted worthy to escape all these things that shall come to pass, and to stand before the Son of man" (Luke 21:36). "For the Son of man is as a man taking a far journey, who left his house, and gave authority to his servants, and to every man his work, and commanded the porter to watch. Watch ye therefore: for ye know not when the master of the house cometh, at even, or at midnight, or at the cockcrowing, or in the morning: Lest coming suddenly he find you sleeping. And what I say unto you I say unto all, Watch" (Mark 13:34–37). "But of that day and that hour knoweth no man, no, not the angels which are in heaven, neither the Son, but the Father. Heaven and earth shall pass away; but my words shall not pass away" (Mark 13:32, 31).

It is with this same definite certainty that I can declare it unto you, on the authority of our Lord Jesus' words and, secondarily, on that of those two Heavenly angel messengers: ". . . Ye men of Galilee, why stand ye gazing up into heaven? this same Jesus, which is taken up from you into heaven, shall so come in like manner as ye have seen him go into heaven" (Acts 1:11). It is in our Bibles that God sets forth this promise: ". . . in the mouth of two or three witnesses every word may be established" (Matthew 18:16). (See also Deuteronomy 19:15; John 8:17–18; 2 Corinthians 13:1; Hebrews 10:28.)

You have been privileged to hear what Jesus, the angelic messengers, Paul, Peter, and John have declared, relative to our Lord's certain return. Jesus' word alone is enough for me! With this in mind, it is appropriate to give you this Scripture from 2 Chronicles 20:20: ". . . Believe in the Lord your God, so shall ye be established; believe his prophets, so shall ye prosper."

It is not possible even to take the Lord's Supper, the Communion service, without conscientiously testifying to our faith in the coming of the Lord Jesus. 1 Corinthians 11: 26 says: "For as often as ye eat this bread, and drink this cup, ye do shew the Lord's death till he come." The Lord ordained that we should take Communion often, for there is a twofold purpose in doing so. One is to anticipate His coming again. The other is to insure the required examination we are supposed to make of our own hearts and our present state of grace, lest we partake unworthily. If we are living in secret sin, we shall be guilty of the body and blood of the Lord, thereby incurring damnation unto ourselves. "For this cause many are weak and sickly . . . and many [spiritually] sleep." This is the warning note which the Holy Spirit gives in 1 Corinthians 11:30, and we will do well to give earnest heed, lest we, too, be condemned with the world. Jesus said: "Behold, I come quickly: hold that fast which thou hast, that no man take thy crown" (Revelation 3:11).

We have emphasized the Lord's "shalls." ". . . yet a little while, and he that shall come will come, and will not tarry." But, from the prophecies of the past, there is also a necessary reminder which I must share. Those who are inclined to become careless and neglectful must note that God said there would be a flood in the days of Noah, and there was! Jesus said: "And as it was in the days of Noe, so shall it be also in the days of the Son of man" (Luke 17:26). God told Abraham that Sodom would be destroyed by fire, and it was! Jesus said: "But the same day that Lot went out of Sodom it rained fire and brimstone from heaven, and destroyed them all. Even thus shall it be in the day when the Son of man is revealed" (Luke 17:29, 30). The positivism of our Lord's coming is set over against the background of these certain prophecies already fulfilled. Thus, Jesus states it in terms simple and plain, in terms we can count on: He is surely and certainly coming again, beyond any shadow of doubt!

And now, I have a final word to those of you who are not yet saved from your sins, who do not know the joy of salvation through faith in our Lord Jesus Christ. In order to be true to your precious, never-dying souls and faithful to bring you the whole counsel of God, I feel that you deserve to know the certainty of what awaits you in the future if you do not repent.

God's "shalls" do mean *shall*, and this is what the Bible declares: "And as it is appointed unto men once to die, and after this the judgment" (Hebrews 9:27). ". . . for we shall all stand before the judgment seat of Christ . . . So then every one of us shall give account of himself to God" (Romans 14:10, 12). And, for all who have refused to come to Jesus for cleansing and pardon, there is a final "shall": "And these shall go away into everlasting punishment: but the righteous into life eternal" (Matthew 25:46).

O precious souls, whom Jesus came into the world to seek and to save from your sins, Jesus is calling you now. "Come unto me, all ye that labour and are heavy laden, and I will give you rest" (Matthew 11:28). ". . . and him that cometh to me I will in no wise cast out" (John 6:37).

I have this good news for you: Despite those "shalls" which denote the certainty of Jesus' coming and the certainty of judgment for the wicked, there is another certain and positive "shall" for the repentant one who turns to Jesus for mercy: "Believe on the Lord Jesus Christ, and thou shalt be saved . . ." (Acts 16: 31). ". . . whosoever shall call on the name of the Lord shall be saved" (Acts 2:21). ". . . thou shalt call his name JESUS: for he shall save his people from their sins" (Matthew 1:21). ". . . All manner of sin and blasphemy shall be forgiven unto men . . ." (Matthew 12:31). ". . . though your sins be as scarlet, they shall be as white as snow; though they be red like crimson, they shall be as wool" (Isaiah 1:18). ". . . He that heareth my word, and believeth on him that sent me, hath everlasting life, and shall not come into condemnation; but is passed from death unto life" (John 5:24). "He that believeth and is baptized shall be saved; but he that believeth not shall be damned (Mark 16:16).